Dandelion Time

A Fantasy

Patricia Wood

A Samuel French Acting Edition

FOUNDED 1830

SAMUELFRENCH-LONDON.CO.UK
SAMUELFRENCH.COM

Copyright © 1993 by Patricia Wood
All Rights Reserved

DANDELION TIME is fully protected under the copyright laws of the British Commonwealth, including Canada, the United States of America, and all other countries of the Copyright Union. All rights, including professional and amateur stage productions, recitation, lecturing, public reading, motion picture, radio broadcasting, television and the rights of translation into foreign languages are strictly reserved.

ISBN 978-0-573-05043-5

www.samuelfrench-london.co.uk

www.samuelfrench.com

FOR AMATEUR PRODUCTION ENQUIRIES

UNITED KINGDOM AND WORLD
EXCLUDING NORTH AMERICA
plays@SamuelFrench-London.co.uk
020 7255 4302/01

Each title is subject to availability from Samuel French,
depending upon country of performance.

CAUTION: Professional and amateur producers are hereby warned that *DANDELION TIME* is subject to a licensing fee. Publication of this play does not imply availability for performance. Both amateurs and professionals considering a production are strongly advised to apply to the appropriate agent before starting rehearsals, advertising, or booking a theatre. A licensing fee must be paid whether the title is presented for charity or gain and whether or not admission is charged.

The professional rights in this play are controlled by Samuel French Ltd, 52 Fitzroy Street, London, W1T 5JR.

No one shall make any changes in this title for the purpose of production. No part of this book may be reproduced, stored in a retrieval system, or transmitted in any form, by any means, now known or yet to be invented, including mechanical, electronic, photocopying, recording, videotaping, or otherwise, without the prior written permission of the publisher. No one shall upload this title, or part of this title, to any social media websites.

The right of Patricia Wood to be identified as author of this work has been asserted by her in accordance with Section 77 of the Copyright, Designs and Patents Act 1988

CHARACTERS

First presented by Hurstpierpoint Players, at Hurstpierpoint College Theatre on January 5th, 1977, with the following cast:

Thomas, 10 years old	Daniel Murray
Josephine, 12 years old	Kate Lummis
Charlotte, 14 years old	Lindsey Buck
The Children's Mother	Christine Page
Mrs Ariadne Time, wife of Father Time	Cicely Lummis
Hickory Dickory Dock, a professional mouse-frightener	Geoffrey Harris
The Parcel Woman	Aileen Smith
Rekelen, an elderly raven	Charles Holding
Frod	John Hughes
Harley	David Patrick
Till — military personnel from	Rick Farmer
Binjer — the planet Pluto	Simon Armes
Dred	Adam Fleming
The Phoenix, a fabled golden bird	Marcia Hughes
Mrs Noah	Barbie Buck
Noah	Don Leonard
Goatnose	Kate Smith
Glumm } Goblins	Caroline Fleming
Gooseberry	Judi Buck
The Goblin Herald	Jeremy Buck
Glinter, King of the Goblins	Simon Murray
The Goose Woman	Margot Allen
The North Wind	David Martin
1st Drowned Sailor	David Campbell
2nd Drowned Sailor	Don Leonard
3rd Drowned Sailor	Ian Cole
Thetis, daughter of King Neptune	Hazel Sellens
1st Sea Maiden	Jacqueline Stock
2nd Sea Maiden	Belinda Fleming
3rd Sea Maiden	Anne Smith
Neptune, King of the Oceans	John Lummis
The Fat Lady	Barbie Buck
Rosie, the bare-back rider	Judi Buck
Esther, the trapeze artiste	Jayne Skinner
Bertha, the bearded lady	Shana Hole

Billiam the Tenth, King of Pluto	Christopher Wood
Glary, Queen of Pluto	Anne Stock
Clerk of the Court	Christopher Clarke
Intercessor	Jill Armstrong
The Judge	Christopher Ayles
The Jailor	John Lummis
The Jailor's Mother	Jane Murray
Father Time	John Stevens

Mice, Sea Cucumbers, Sea People, Goblins, Plutonians, Circus Folk and Time Troglodytes

The Play directed by Patricia Wood

Several of these characters may be doubled, please see page v

ACT I
- SCENE 1   An upstairs room in a London house
- SCENE 2   The Clock Labyrinth
- SCENE 3   The Slopes of Mount Ararat
- SCENE 4   The Land of the Goblins

ACT II
- SCENE 1   The Land of Limbo
- SCENE 2   Beneath the Ocean
- SCENE 3   A Circus Ring
- SCENE 4   The Planet Pluto
- SCENE 5   The Clock Labyrinth

SETTINGS

These consist mainly of seven large cubes, each with its six faces painted to represent a different scene, like a child's box of bricks. The cubes are moved into various positions in a penumbra of light by the Time Troglodytes. Backing and wing flats should be black, or of some dark colour.

NOTES ON THE CHARACTERS

Mrs Ariadne Time: She is a small figure dressed in bright, flouncy skirts and petticoats in many vivid patterns. She wears a lacy, silver shawl around her shoulders and her tumbling pale curls are tied with red and yellow ribbons. At first glance she might be a young girl, but a closer look shows us that the bright cheeks are heavily rouged and the lips and eyes carefully painted. This girlish figure is at least two million years old.

Hickory Dickory Dock: A mouse-frightener by trade. He wears trousers and a jacket striped and checked in brilliant shades of green and purple. A small round leather hat is on his head and a large leather apron with a capacious pocket is around his waist. A whistle hangs around his neck.

The Parcel Woman: She is neatly dressed in a brown skirt decorated with Christmas labels and stamps. The bodice is tied together with bows of string, and the whole costume is finished by an apron made from today's *The Times*.

The Goblins (Goatnose, Glumm and Gooseberry): They wear yellow-and-brown jackets and trousers, bright blue caps and little blue cloaks. They are fat with round red cheeks, high clear voices and white beards.

The Goose Woman: Her grey hair is wispy and soft and her clothes are the dull greys and yellows of a snow cloud. The odd goose feather clings to her hair and to the hem of her dress.

Thetis: The daughter of King Neptune. She is very beautiful but rather bad tempered, and clad in floating green garments, lavishly decorated with pearls and corals.

King Neptune: He has a long white beard, sea-weedy hair and blue cloak, all of which billow about him in the sea. Various sea-creatures cling about his garments and his gleaming trident and crown are hung about with sea worms and star-fish.

Other characters are dealt with as they appear in the text.

Suggestions for doubling of characters:

Children's mother, Mrs Noah and The Fat Lady
Mrs Ariadne Time, The Goose Woman and Rosie
The Parcel Woman and Esther
Noah, King Neptune and Father Time (It is also possible for this actor to play King Glinter and The Bearded Lady, to good effect)
Gooseberry, 1st Drowned Sailor and Clerk of the Court

Glumm, 2nd Drowned Sailor, and Intercessor
Goatnose, 3rd Drowned Sailor and Jailor
Thetis and Queen Glary
North Wind and King Billiam
King Glinter, Judge and Ringmaster
A small group can double all the extras, i.e. mice, goblins, etc.

ACT I

Scene 1

A room on the first floor of a Victorian house in London. The time is the present. It is about 4.30 on a November afternoon, and a street lamp shines in through the window which is down stage right in the fourth wall. Two of the cubes pushed together indicate a window seat. At the back and left of centre stands a large grandfather clock with the figures on its face in all the wrong positions. Centre right is a round table covered with a dark cloth. At this table the three children are playing a very noisy game of Ludo. The room is gloomy and only their top halves are visible to the audience. The rest of them is hidden in the gloom and concealed as well as possible by the folds of the tablecloth.

Thomas (*shouting wildly*) A six, a six! I've got another six! I'll soon be home!
Josephine (*crossly*) You didn't shake it—you just *tipped* it out! I saw you! You're *always* doing that!
Thomas I didn't, I shook it like anything! Didn't I, Charley?
Charlotte You didn't shake it much!
Josephine He didn't shake it at all!
Thomas Oh, yes I did! You're annoyed because I'm winning!
Josephine Be quiet, and get on with the game!
Thomas (*counting at the top of his voice*) One, two, three, four, five, six—I'm nearly home! (*Thumping his fist on the table*) I'm nearly home!!
Charlotte Look out, you'll have the board over, Thomas. And give me that—it's my turn!

She takes the cup and dice

Josephine Make sure you shake it properly. No tipping out!

Charlotte makes a face at Josephine, and holding the cup in the air she shakes the dice in an exaggerated way. While she is shaking it a hand-bell sounds loudly from the street, and a man's voice is heard calling. The three Ludo players seem not to hear this

Josephine Come on, Charley! Don't be so stupid!
Thomas You'll shake the spots off!
Charlotte (*tipping the dice out*) Two. I haven't moved for *ages*.

She hands the cup to her sister who shakes it vigorously

Josephine (*triumphantly*) Six!—Now, shall I move that one, or get another out?

The three gaze at the board while Josephine thinks. The bell in the street sounds again, louder. The Man's voice is louder, too, but the words are drowned in a rattle of cart wheels and horses' hooves. The Ludo players still do not hear any of this

Charlotte Hurry up, Jo, it's nearly tea-time.
Thomas Yes, hurry up, I want to see the cartoon on television.
Josephine Go on then, nobody's stopping you.
Thomas But I want to see who wins!
Josephine You'll win because you cheat!
Thomas (*hotly*) I *don't* cheat!
Josephine Yes you do!
Thomas (*furiously*) No I don't!!

The children's Mother has entered from the shadows

Mother What a very noisy game. I hope it's nearly finished because we want the table for tea. And why did you not light the lamp?

Their mother moves down to the window and we see that she is wearing a long Edwardian tea-gown, with her hair piled softly on top of her head

Charlotte We may as well pack up.
Thomas You'd never have won anyway, Charley.
Josephine I think Ludo's a silly game.

They are busy packing the game into the box

Charlotte (*looking up suddenly*) Mother, did you say "light the lamp"?
Mother (*gazing out of the window as though looking for something*) Of course. It's so bad for your eyes playing a game in this gloom.
Charlotte (*utterly mystified*) But Mother—"light the *lamp*"?
Mother (*placidly*) Yes, dear. You know, I could be sure I heard the muffin man in the road, but I can't see him anywhere.

All three are now looking at her in astonishment

Josephine The *muffin* man?
Mother Yes, dear. I thought muffins would be nice for tea. It's such a gloomy afternoon.
Thomas Why are you wearing that long dress? You never wear a long dress in the afternoons. Are you going out tonight? You've done your hair all different!

As Thomas speaks we hear the sound of a horse and carriage drawing up outside

Mother Goodness, there's Father. He's home early, I must go down. (*She looks at the children*) Clear the table, wash your hands and brush your hair. You look like savages.

She disappears into the shadows. The children look after her in astonishment. Charlotte goes to the window seat, kneels on it and looks down

Act I, Scene 1

Charlotte (*astonished at what she sees*) It's a kind of carriage with a horse pulling it. And Father's wearing his evening suit with a top hat! I can't see any more, he's come in through the front door!
Thomas (*utterly shattered*) Brush our hair? For *tea*? Nobody's coming, are they?
Josephine (*coming down to the window and staring at Charlotte*) But, Charley, you're like it too!—Why have you got that stupid dress on? I thought you were wearing your jeans?

Charlotte looks down at herself and realizes that she is in Edwardian dress. Then she looks at Josephine

Charlotte Well, what about you? (*They gaze at themselves in astonishment*) And I've never seen anything like those knee things that Thomas is wearing!
Thomas (*still harping on*) Brush our *hair*?—Why did she say that?
Charlotte (*trying to make him listen*) Thomas!!!
Thomas *Is* anyone coming?
Josephine (*shouting*) Thomas!
Thomas Well, but we *never* brush our hair for tea unless somebody's coming!
Josephine }
Charlotte } (*shrieking at him*) THOMAS!!
Thomas (*paying attention at last*) What?
Josephine Look at yourself!

Thomas sees the clothes he is wearing

Thomas (*shattered*) Oh, crikey!—I *hope* nobody's coming!
Charlotte What a very odd thing to have happened!
Josephine I don't remember putting on these clothes. And we've nothing like them in the dressing-up box. And look at the clock! Just *look* at the clock!

For the first time they notice the figures on the clock face

Charlotte But—it's all wrong!
Josephine *Isn't* it just!
Thomas The figures are in all the wrong places!
Josephine That's what I mean.
Thomas (*getting very excited*) Yes, they are!—There's the ten next to the four, and the five ...
Charlotte What's gone wrong with everything?
Thomas The five's next to the twelve, and the seven is over on the other side next to——
Josephine Oh, shut up, Thomas! We can see all that for ourselves!
Charlotte But what's gone *wrong*? That's what *I* want to know!

The grandfather clock suddenly chimes the half hour all the wrong way round, and out of the shadows by the clock comes Mrs Ariadne Time

Mrs Ariadne (*moving out of the shadows*) *Every*thing's wrong, my dear child! Everything!—And when you've said that, you've said it all!

The children stare at her in astonishment. Then Charlotte, remembering what is due to a visitor, comes forward

Charlotte I'm sorry, we didn't know anyone was here.

Mrs Ariadne Of course not, my dear girl. Naturally. You've got *your* worries, I've got *mine*! It's only to be expected when you think that we come from different sides of the clock. I'm in among the pendulums and cog-wheels, and *you're* out with the digits and the decorations, so to speak.

Thomas Did you come from inside the clock?

Mrs Ariadne That's a plain question. And it deserves a plain answer.

Thomas Well—*did* you come from inside the clock?

Mrs Ariadne Somebody should tell that boy that it's not polite to ask the same question twice. (*She wipes her eyes with a corner of the silver scarf and turns to Charlotte*) Might I sit down, my dear? It won't be like home, but no doubt it will be better than nothing.

Charlotte (*moving a chair forward and helping Mrs Ariadne into it*) I'm so sorry.

Mrs Ariadne (*sitting bolt upright in the chair*) I thought so. Just as I thought. Not a flicker of a movement. (*Loudly*) This chair is remaining perfectly still!

Josephine That's what a chair is supposed to do.

Mrs Ariadne Not on the inside of the clock, it isn't! Everything in there is on the move, you know. A gentle, restful movement. A well-oiled, well-regulated movement. A soft, rhythmical tick—tock, tick—tock . . .

Thomas Not any more, the clock's stopped!

Mrs Ariadne (*bursting into tears*) Oh, what a horrid boy to remind me! Oh, what a nasty, unkind, thoughtless boy! As if I didn't know that it's stopped!—Everything has stopped!—Time is at a standstill—and all because he's gone!

Josephine Who's gone?

Mrs Ariadne Father Time, of course! My dear, *dear*, husband! All is upside down, and topsy-turvy. Two rashers and a fried egg for his breakfast, and there they are congealing on the plate! Gone forever—and the whole world in perplexity!

She sobs bitterly. The children stand helpless, not knowing what to do. The clock chimes again, a very muddled three-quarters, and out of it steps Hickory carrying the Black Time Box

Hickory Now then, Mrs Ariadne, not crying again?

Mrs Ariadne I'm afraid so, Dock.

Hickory It won't help, Mrs Ariadne. It won't do any good. Have you told them?

Mrs Ariadne Yes, I've told them. And what good does *that* do? They just stand there like graven images!

Act I, Scene 1

Hickory (*to Charlotte*) This is no use, you know. We need your help. You must bustle about! Time may stand still but we can't afford to. Now, let's start by introducing ourselves. This is Mrs Ariadne Time, wife of Father Time.

This brings forth a fresh burst of sobbing from Mrs Ariadne

Now don't cry any more, there's a good soul. We need all our resources, and you *know* how it rusts up the works. (*He turns to the children and holds out his hand.*) Who are you?

The children in turn tell Hickory their names and shake hands with him

Good. I'm Hickory, surname Dock, middle name Dickory.

Thomas You mean like the mouse who ran up the clock?

Hickory Not that old joke again, please! The mouse who ran up the clock was just any old mouse. In fact, lots of mice! They do it all the time, you know. *I'm* Hickory Dickory Dock. And I'm a mouse-frightener by trade. Mice have to be kept out of the works, you know, they'd do untold damage if left inside a clock.

Thomas How do you frighten them?

Hickory Do you really want me to show you?

Thomas Yes, please.

Not displeased with the chance to show off, Hickory goes into his mouse-frightening routine. This consists of tremendous contortions of the face, yelling, stamping and blowing the whistle. When finished he mops his face

Hickory Exhausting work.

Thomas That's very good. I should think it would frighten any mouse.

Hickory Oh, it does. Scares them out of their wits. But this won't do, you know. We, that is, you, me and Mrs Ariadne here, we've got to find Father Time.

Charlotte What's happened to him?

Hickory (*in a sepulchral tone*) Kidnapped!!

Josephine Really?

Hickory What else? Father Time is a national figure. Worldwide renown, and all that! You know what the world is like nowadays, we are all surrounded by danger! It's there in the shadows, waiting and watching! Why, they might take me next!

Mrs Ariadne (*bridling*) Don't give yourself airs, Dock. Remember you're only an employee. An underling.

Thomas What's an underling?

Mrs Ariadne Somebody should tell that boy to stop asking questions. He's wasting time!

Hickory And there's precious little of it left. (*He taps the time box*) Just enough to get us all into the back of the clock. You see, when Time stops, everything stops. No-one can move from place to place. Everything stays just as it is.

Thomas *We* didn't! We got put into these ridiculous clothes!

Josephine Yes, and Father came home in a horse and carriage!

Hickory That was my fault, really. I do apologize. You see, when we realized the emergency, I opened the Time Box, which has a bit of reserve time in it, and I let out too much. Everything slipped back a bit.
Charlotte Can you put it right?
Hickory Only Father Time can do that. So we *must* find him. You will help us, won't you?
Josephine Of course we will.
Thomas But how can we search for Father Time if everything is at a standstill?
Mrs Ariadne There he goes again! Questions, questions!
Hickory (*holding up the black wooden box*) We've got a little reserve time left in the Time Box. It's enough to get us into the Works Department at the back of the clock, and there we'll make our plans.
Charlotte I hope it won't take too long because it's almost tea-time, and Mother will be wanting the table laid.
Mrs Ariadne There won't be any tea-time, my dear. Nor supper time, nor going to bed time, not while he's gone. (*She sobs again*)
Thomas No going to bed time? I like the sound of that.
Hickory Well, come on, if you're coming. (*He opens the door of the clock*) Down the steps and mind your heads on the pendulum.

They go into the clock. Mrs Ariadne first, followed by the children. Hickory is last in and is just about to close the door when a row of Mice advances out of the shadows towards the clock, dancing and squeaking in the light from the street lamp. In a second Hickory is out of the clock and into his mouse-frightening routine. The Mice watch it through to the end, mesmerized by the noise and awfulness of it. Then they flee, shrieking. Hickory mops his brow

Hickory And now for the last bit of time to get us into the Clock Labyrinth.

He opens the box and the last little bit of time wriggles out. The loudest clock in the world begins to tick in a slow and laboured way. The music of time itself starts to play as if on an old run down gramophone. Hickory disappears through the clock door just as the Time Troglodytes whirl it away into blackness. Swiftly they move the great cubes until they are settled into the pattern of the clock labyrinth. The trogs melt away, and Mrs Ariadne, the children and Hickory appear in the passage just as the clock gives its last, laboured tick. The music of time ceases, and all is silent and still

SCENE 2

THE CLOCK LABYRINTH

Charlotte How quiet it is.
Josephine And still.
Mrs Ariadne It will be until *he* comes back. No sound. No movement. Not the flicker of an eyelid. Not the breath of a snail. Here we are, and here we shall stay.

Act I, Scene 2

Thomas I don't want to stay here, it's too boring. Just bits of insides of clocks. What's down there? (*He points to a dark and shadowy part of the labyrinth*)
Hickory That leads to other worlds, and other times.
Charlotte And what's that noise I can hear? I thought at first it was the clock starting again.
Josephine So did I. But it's more a clicking kind of noise.

They listen. There is a clicking noise coming from somewhere close at hand.

Mrs Ariadne (*sulkily*) That'll be her with her everlasting knitting. Everlastingly knitting she is. On and on—click—click—click. It gets on my nerves, that everlasting click—click—click!
Charlotte Who is it?
Mrs Ariadne The Parcel Woman, that's who it is. She's here somewhere. You can tell by the click—click—click. It gets on my nerves, that everlasting click—click—click. (*Raising her voice*) Stop that, you Parcel Woman, you! Stop that everlasting click—click—click!

The clicking stops and the Parcel Woman appears at the top of a cube. She has a long piece of knitting in her hand

Parcel Woman Somebody call me?
Mrs Ariadne I called out to you to stop that click—click—click! That's why I called out to you, you Parcel Woman!
Parcel Woman Ah. It sounds louder now the clock has stopped. Any sign of him yet?
Hickory None.
Parcel Woman I thought not. The world is in a muddle now, I've heard. Where's he gone to?
Hickory Kidnapped, *I* think.
Parcel Woman Shouldn't wonder. Not with things as they are.—What are these? (*She points a knitting-needle towards the children*)
Hickory Children.
Parcel Woman They look like graven images.
Hickory That's because they can't move much, you see, we've run out of time. They're going to help us look for him.
Parcel Woman That's all right, but *where* will you look?
Hickory Here and there.
Parcel Woman That won't do. You must be positive. I'll call Rekelen. He goes about. Rekelen sees things—he notices. (*She calls a harsh cawing cry*)
Charlotte Who's Rekelen?
Mrs Ariadne A raven. A mangy, moth-eaten old raven. What good is that?
Hickory He goes about in the air where everything is different. He has advantages. We must not despise any help, Mrs Ariadne. The crisis is too great.

Rekelen arrives at the top of a cube. He is indeed a moth-eaten old raven.

Parcel Woman Now, Rekelen, your help is needed. Father Time is lost, gone, vanished, disappeared!

Mrs Ariadne (*annoyed*) I'll tell it, if you don't mind, Parcel Woman! (*She turns to Rekelen*) I was just cooking Father Time's breakfast—I'm his wife, you see, we've been married for hundreds of years—well, I'd got the bacon in the pan, and the egg broke in a cup——

Hickory (*interrupting*) It won't do, Mrs Ariadne! This is not the moment for a long story. (*He turns briskly to Rekelen*) Father Time is missing. Kidnapped is *my* belief. We *must* get him back at once. Have you seen him?

Rekelen (*yawning*) Describe.

Hickory Long white beard—*very* long, down to here. White hair, grey eyes, white tunic, blue cloak. Carries a scythe. Never without it.

Rekelen Age?

Mrs Ariadne Middle-aged, quite young.

Hickory Over a billion years, I should think. Though he doesn't look it.

Mrs Ariadne (*obstinately*) Middle-aged. Older than me, of course.

Rekelen (*after scratching his head and thinking for a moment or two*) Top of a mountain. Early this morning. Old man. Long white beard. Something in his hand glittering in the sun.

Hickory (*excitedly*) The scythe! It *must* be him! They've kidnapped him and left him stranded at the top of a mountain. Crafty devils! Can you take us?

Rekelen puts his head on one side

Rekelen Can you fly?

Hickory No.

Rekelen Then I can't. What about these? (*He points to the children*)

Hickory They're children. They can't fly.

Rekelen They look more like graven images.

Hickory If only we had a way of moving time just for a moment or two. Then we could follow Rekelen to the mountain.

Parcel Woman What about the Time Box?

Hickory Empty.

Mrs Ariadne (*sobbing*) It's all over. All finished. The world will never move again!

Charlotte Don't cry, Mrs Ariadne. We'll think of something.

Josephine All we need is a way to move time on just a little bit.

Thomas (*with sudden inspiration*) Dandelions!

Hickory
Mrs Ariadne } *What?*
Parcel Woman

Thomas Dandelion clocks!—You blow them to tell the time!

Mrs Ariadne Take no notice of that boy. That's a very badly behaved boy, that is.

Hickory What do you tell time?

Thomas Whatever you like, I should think. We could blow the dandelion clocks and then tell time where we wanted to go!

Act I, Scene 2   9

Hickory (*excitedly*) We'll try it!—Where are these dandelion clocks?
Charlotte Oh, Thomas, but it's winter. We'd never find any dandelion clocks *now*!
Josephine Besides, it's only a game!
Hickory I want to try it! We must try everything!
Charlotte But where are we going to find dandelion clocks at this time of year?
Parcel Woman I might be able to help you there. I might have some in a parcel in my cupboard, you know. I keep everything, and I keep nothing, all wrapped up in brown paper parcels. I've got parcels of cobwebs, parcels of breadcrumbs, parcels of lizards tails. Have you ever seen a lizard's tail that a cat has bitten off?—Well, I *might* have dandelion clocks in a parcel, in my cupboard.
Josephine Then please won't you go and look?
Parcel Woman You must help. There are so many parcels, I can't do it alone.
Hickory We'll all go.
Mrs Ariadne I'm not going into the Parcel Woman's dusty old cupboard. I'll go back into the clock and wait. That's all that's left to me now, waiting.
Hickory That's right, Mrs Ariadne, you go back and make a nice cup of tea. That'll be a comfort to you, and we'll come as soon as we can and tell you how we've got on!

Mrs Ariadne sobs her way back to the clock, while Hickory, the children and Rekelen follow the Parcel Woman off to her cupboard. For a moment the labyrinth is absolutely quiet. Then the silence is broken by a clattering noise, like tins being knocked together, and voices loudly hushing one another. The clattering sound comes closer and closer

Harley (*calling from somewhere in the labyrinth*) All right?—I say, Frod! Are you all right?

The clattering stops

Frod What?
Harley Are you all right, Frod?
Frod (*calling back*) Course I am!—(*Clank, clatter*) I'm nearly there! (*Laboured breathing*)—I am there!!! (*Very loud clanking and clattering*)

A strange figure has appeared on top of one of the cubes. It is clad in a shiny, silvery suit, and has very large ears. Perched on top of its head is a tweed cap, and it is liberally hung about with tin cans

Frod I'm there!!—I say—I'm *THERE!!*

The silver figure waves its arms triumphantly and, with a deafening clatter, falls from the cube to the ground. There is a moment's silence, and then an anxious voice calls from back in the labyrinth

Harley Frod!!
Frod What?
Harley You all right?
Frod 'Course I am. (*A tentative clanking among the tins*) But I've lost the tin-opener.

Harley, also clad in silver and wearing a tweed cap, enters and looks towards the heap of tins which is Frod

Harley You done what?
Frod (*slightly exasperated*) Lost the tin-opener!—Help me up, can't you?
Harley (*calling back to his companions*) He's gone and lost the tin-opener!

Three more silver persons come out of the shadows

Till What's he done?
Harley (*helping the pile of tins to its feet*) Lost the tin-opener.
Till He never had the tin-opener, Harley.
Harley Never *had* it?
Till No. Binjer's got the tin-opener.
Binjer That's right. I got the tin-opener, Harley.
Harley I thought it was you had the torch?
Binjer No, Harley. I never had the torch. Dred had the torch.
Harley Is that right, Dred? You had the torch?
Dred That's right, Harley.
Harley Then switch it on, I can't see a thing.
Dred I can't switch it on, Harley.
Harley How's that?
Dred I left it behind.
Harley In't it marvellous? Planned down to the last detail, this operation was. Months it took us to learn the language! We got the right gear, we got the right provisions, we got ourselves beamed down to earth at the right moment, and Dred goes and leaves the torch behind!
Dred Sorry, Harley.
Harley How are we going to find this Earth lot what we're supposed to be following, without the torch?
Till We could do it by touch, Harley.
Harley (*disgustedly*) Do it by touch!—Frod did it by touch, and look where it got him!
Frod (*who has been examining his tins*) I seem to have crushed the baked beans, Harley.
Harley (*really exasperated*) Never mind the baked beans! Pull yourselves together! This is a military expedition sent to Earth by His Majesty the King of Pluto!—You lot are supposed to be trained to a hair! Get in line!!

They do so

Now then, let's have the Plutonian Battle Cry. And put a bit of go into it!

Act I, Scene 2   11

All Yes, Harley.
Harley Then—One, two, three, GO!!

And suiting the actions to the words the Plutonians give forth their battle cry

Plutonians With—a—
    One two, left right,
    Clap three, stamp four,
    WE ARE FROM PLUTO!
    Left right, clap five!
    Brave and daring, from the sky
    Sounds the Plutonian Battle Cry!!

As the brave Plutonians finish their battle cry, the voice of Mrs Ariadne Time is heard screaming in the labyrinth

Mrs Ariadne (*in the distance*) Help, Help! They've got in!! Where are you, Dock? Help, help!!
Binjer That's an Earth Person's voice, Harley.
Harley You're right, Binjer. We'll melt quietly away into the shadows.

They melt quietly away, all except Frod, who clanks

Harley (*in a loud whisper*) Watch the noise, Frod!
Frod Sorry, Harley.

Frod clanks off into the shadows. Mrs Ariadne Time rushes on, shrieking. She climbs on to a cube and holds her skirts above her knees. She is followed by a crowd of Mice, who, squeaking gleefully, surround her cube

Mrs Ariadne (*at the top of her voice*) Dock!!—They're here!!—They've got in!! Do your duty, Dock! I'm surrounded!! There are hundreds of them—millions of them—the whole place is awash with them!! Help!! HELP!!! *Where—are—you—Dock???*

Hickory hurries back, breathless and panting

Hickory Here I am, Mrs Ariadne! Don't you panic!—Oh, my goodness, the little devils!—(*He fixes the mice with his eye*) Now then—*you*!!

Hickory gives a particularly effective rendering of his mouse-frightening routine. As before, they watch him in petrified silence, and then run off panic-striken

Mrs Ariadne (*a nervous wreck*) I can't stand it, Dock. Mice flooding into the main springs, and eating the fried eggs off his very plate. (*She sits on her cube weeping into the silver scarf*) I'm finished! I can't go on without him! It's too much to bear. No-one should *expect* me to bear it. Loneliness at *my* age, Dock? It's unthinkable! It's against nature, that's what it is. I'm nothing but a poor, innocent creature swept away on the tides of despair. (*She stands on her cube, flinging out her arms*) This is the end, Dock!—You do as you like! Loosen the main spring, sell up the jewels and go off somewhere by yourself. Just leave me here to die—that's all I ask!

Hickory Come now, Mrs Ariadne, this won't do!! Cheer up! We've got the answer to the problem!—*What* do you think the Parcel Woman has found for us—eh?

Mrs Ariadne (*sniffing*) I don't know, Dock. Some obnoxious substance, I have no doubt.

Hickory Dandelion clocks, Mrs Ariadne! Think of that! Five dandelion clocks!

Mrs Ariadne *And* a lot of dust, if appearances is to be believed!

Hickory Five dandelion clocks in good condition. The others are bringing them along now. Why, Mrs Ariadne, we'll be off to the top of that mountain and back here with Father Time, before the tears on your face have dried!

The three children, followed by Rekelen and the Parcel Woman, come in. She carries an opened brown paper parcel. Rekelen goes straight to a cube and roosts.

Josephine (*running to Mrs Ariadne*) We've got them! Isn't that wonderful? Five Dandelion clocks!

Charlotte Oh, Jo, I don't see *how* it can work!

Thomas Of course it can work. Anything can happen here, I should think. Why, fancy us being in the back of the grandfather clock!—*That's* something you might think could never happen!

Hickory There's been enough talk, and now the thing must be tried. Everyone who is going to the top of the mountain take one dandelion clock!

The three children take one each. Josephine hands one to Hickory

Thomas (*holding up the last one*) This one is spare.

Charlotte That's for Mrs Ariadne.

Mrs Ariadne Not me, my dear. I'm staying here. I'll die if I must, but I'll die comfortable and in my own place.

Thomas What about Rekelen?

Parcel Woman A raven has its own time, boy. A raven moves in the upper streams of air. A raven is alert to the winds of change, and ready to make use of currents and eddies and such.

Rekelen snores loudly and changes his head to the other wing

Josephine (*to the Parcel Woman*) Won't you come with us?

Parcel Woman I don't leave the clock labyrinth. Nor do I leave my parcels. Nor do I leave my knitting.

Mrs Ariadne That's right, *she'll* stay! I say, *she'll* stay, that Parcel Woman will—with her everlasting click—click—click!

Hickory I'll take the spare dandelion clock in the Time Box in case of necessity. Wake Rekelen, and we'll try for some dandelion time.

Act I, Scene 2   13

Thomas gives Rekelen a little dig, The raven wakes with a disgruntled croak

Mrs Ariadne Somebody should tell that boy that it's not polite to dig a person when a person is asleep!
Rekelen (*smoothing down his feathers*) If we do not make haste, the mountain will be on the move before *we* can move Time!
Thomas We hold the dandelion clocks up like this, and blow on them. Then, when some of the little white seeds blow off, we can tell time.
Hickory Are you ready?

They hold up the dandelion clocks and look upstage towards Rekelen, who is as ready to lead them as a moth-eaten raven can be

One—two—three—BLOW!!

The dandelion clock holders blow hard, but nothing happens

Charlotte I *told* you!
Thomas Don't fuss, Charley. We must blow harder. Mrs Ariadne! You and the Parcel Woman must help!
Hickory Ready to try again?—One—two—three—BLOW!!

All of them blow very hard indeed. In fact, the Parcel Woman is quite red in the face with her efforts, but still nothing happens

Charlotte I *told* you! (*She sits down disconsolately*)
Thomas Don't keep *saying* that!!
Josephine Oh, *why* won't it work?
Thomas We're not blowing hard enough, that's why.
Parcel Woman Difficult to blow into a still and heavy air. Like pushing against a steel door that never opens.
Thomas We must get more people to blow. There aren't enough of us.
Parcel Woman The whole world should help. The whole world *uses* time when it's there to be used, so it should help to get it back.
Mrs Ariadne The world is in perplexity, you Parcel Woman, you. How can the world help?
Parcel Woman It can blow, I should think?
Hickory So it can, and so it must! I'll ask it. (*He turns round and round looking for it*) Where is it?
Rekelen If I am not mistaken it appears to be out there.

Rekelen waves a tattered wing in the direction of the audience. The people in the labyrinth turn and look out at it

Parcel Woman (*peering out*) That's it, is it? Out there?
Rekelen Out there, yes.
Parcel Woman Looks like nothing more nor less than a lot of graven images.
Rekelen It may give that impression because it is sitting still and doing nothing.
Mrs Ariadne (*grumbling*) That's just like the world, to sit still and do nothing. Just like it, when there's everything at stake.

Hickory (*stepping forward and addressing the world*) If you can hear me, world, will you please help?—Time has stopped and we must move it on with the dandelion clocks so that Rekelen can take us to the top of the mountain. Father Time *must* be found and brought back again! If you are going to help, would you please nod your heads like this. (*He nods*)

Josephine (*standing beside him*) Are they nodding?

Hickory (*shading his eyes*) I think so. Some of them are. Yes, quite a lot of them are! Now, world, when I count one-two-three, please blow as hard as you can. Are you ready? Then, one—two—three—BLOW!!!

All the people in the labyrinth blow as hard as they can, and the world blows as well. A few dandelion seeds begin to float in the air

Hickory (*wildly excited*) It's starting, it's starting!!! To the mountain!!

A slow laboured tick is heard, and the music of time begins to sound across the universe. The children and Hickory are whirled round and round as they follow Rekelen out. The time Troglodytes move the great cubes, the seeds fall to the earth, the slow ticking ceases, and the music of time is silent. A bright sunshiny light breaks over the top of the mountain

SCENE 3

THE SLOPES OF MOUNT ARARAT

From lower down the mountain comes the sound of men marching, and the strains of the Plutonian battle cry fall upon the ear, accompanied by the rattle of tins

Plutonians One two, left right,
Clap three, stamp four,
WE ARE FROM PLUTO!
Left right, clap five!
Brave and daring, from the sky
Sounds the Plutonian Battle Cry!!

They appear, marching in a rather ragged line with Harley bringing up the rear

Harley Company—HALT!

It does so

Harley On the command "Fall out" the Company will fall out!—Company—"FALL OUT"!

They do so

Act I, Scene 3   15

Harley On the command "Scatter" the Company will scatter and search for twigs and dried branches to make a impenetrable barricade against sudden and unwarranted attacks by the enemy.
Till What are they, Harley?
Harley What are what?
Till The enemy.
Harley We shall know that, Till, when they makes a sudden and unwarranted attack.
Dred When will they do that, Harley?
Harley According to Company Orders, they are not likely to do that until after the barricade is finished.
Frod Why?
Harley Why what?
Frod Why are they not likely to do what you said they wasn't?
Harley (*looking at Frod with some dislike*) Because, being short of time, they moves slower than what we do. Now hold your noise, Frod, and let's get on!
Frod Sorry, Harley.
Harley (*in his parade ground voice*) For the purpose of searching for twigs and dried branches to make a impenetrable barrier—Company—SCATTER!!!

The Company scatters a trifle unwillingly, with many a Plutonian grumble. Binjer peers behind a cube, down left, pulls a twig from behind it, and takes it to Harley

Binjer Excuse me, Harley, is this a twig or dried branch?
Harley (*examining the find*) Well done, Binjer! That is a twig!!
Binjer There's a whole pile of them behind that lump of rock, Harley.
Harley I shall mention you in despatches for this, Binjer. Company—FALL IN!!!

They do so

Harley Binjer here has found a supply of twigs. On the command "Pass Twigs" they shall be passed from hand to hand, and the work of making a impenetrable barricade will commence. Company!—PASS TWIGS!!

Binjer goes to the side of the rock and starts handing out twigs. These are passed down the line until they reach the end and are then put into a pile. They have passed quite a few down the line, singing the Plutonian battle cry to keep up a rhythm, when a loud cry of fury stops them in their tracks

On top of the cube from behind which Binjer has been taking the twigs stands the Phoenix. Its golden eyes ablaze. Its golden feathers quivering with rage!

Phoenix How *dare* you!—How *dare* you!!! This desecration must cease! Do you understand? CEASE!!—I command you at once to drop the twigs that belong to the sacred funeral pyre of the Phoenix, or I shall be forced to encompass and consume you with my immortal flames!!

The Plutonians stand transfixed, their mouths open, their eyes wide. The Phoenix comes down from its cube and sweeps across in front of them

Phoenix Vile creatures though ye be, I may yet spare your miserable lives if you at once repair the havoc you have wreaked!!
Frod (*in a hoarse whisper*) Harley?
Harley Yes, Frod?
Frod What's that bird on about?
Harley I dunno, Frod, but we won't take no chances. Company!!—DROP TWIGS!!!

The Plutonians do so

Phoenix That is well done. And now that you may make some reparation for your deed, and thus escape an awful punishment, you will raise your wings towards the heavens, and repeat the ancient hymn of praise to my wonder and majesty!
Harley (*anxious to please*) Company!—RAISE WINGS!!

The Plutonians raise their arms

Phoenix (*who floats backwards and forwards in front of them, in a kind of ecstatic dance*)
   Oh, Phoenix of the golden eye,
   Who on the funeral pyre doth lie,
   With beating wings to burn and die!
  (*To the Plutonians, severely*) Repeat after me! Oh hail, great bird!
Plutonians Oh hail great bird!
Phoenix Oh hail to thee!
Plutonians Oh hail to thee!
Phoenix Fashioned for immortality!
Plutonians Fashioned for immortality!
Phoenix Oh Phoenix of the scented breath,
   Of whom the Eastern Prophet saith
   She is immutable in death!
  (*The Phoenix raises its wing warningly*) Oh hail, great bird!
Plutonians Oh hail, great bird!
Phoenix Oh hail . . .

The voice of the Phoenix, who has been capering about in front of Binjer, ceases with a loud grunt, and the golden bird falls to the ground like a stone. The Plutonians gaze at it in amazement.

Harley Binjer?—What did you do?
Binjer (*a trifle self-consciously*) Nothing much, Harley. I just tapped it on the head with the tin-opener.
Harley Good lad! I'll recommend you for the Plutonian Cross when we get back. And now, we'll melt quietly away into the scenery.

They melt quietly away, all except Frod, who clanks

Act I, Scene 3 17

Harley (*off, in a loud whisper*) Watch the noise, Frod!
Frod Sorry, Harley.

Frod clanks off

The Phoenix lies still, its beak and toes pointing to the sky, and its wings outstretched

Over the top of the mountain comes Mrs Noah with a basket of washing on her arm. She is singing happily

Mrs Noah (*singing*) Oh, it ain't gonna rain no more, no more!
It ain't gonna rain no more!
How in the world can anybody tell
That it ain't gonna rain no more?

She puts the basket down and is about to spread her washing out to dry when she notices the Phoenix, who is still lying deeply unconscious

Mrs Noah Oh, my goodness, gracious me, what's this?—A pigeon?—No, it's the wrong size for a pigeon. A duck, then?—No, the feet don't look right for a duck. Perhaps it's a turkey? Oh, that *would* be nice, that would! A turkey for supper!—Dead, too, by the look of it. How convenient. Roast turkey and cranberry sauce. With lots of gravy, and mashed turnips. I *do* like a mashed turnip with turkey. (*She views the Phoenix from all angles*) I'll need a basket. No, it's too big for a basket. I'll get a rope and drag it up to the ark that's what I'll do!—Oh, what a day. I shall get the washing dry for the first time in years, and we'll have turkey for supper!

She disappears over the top of the mountain, and we hear her calling as she goes:

Noah!—Noah!!—Fetch a bit of rope, will you?—I said FETCH A BIT OF ROPE!!!

Mrs Noah's voice fades into the distance. The Phoenix continues to lie prone upon the ground. Voices can be heard coming up the side of the mountain

Josephine (*who sounds rather out of breath*) Wait, Thomas, don't go so fast!

Thomas appears, flushed and triumphant

Thomas (*calling back to the girls*) It's the top! We've reached it! Rekelen and Hickory haven't come up from the other side yet—we're first!—But I can't see anyone who looks like Father Time.
Josephine (*appearing*) Oh, it's so hot and tiring climbing in this stupid dress!—Come on, Charley, we're at the top!
Thomas (*looking around him*) I wonder what these old bits of wood are doing up here?

Charlotte (*the last to reach the top*) What a *view*! Have you looked at the view, Jo?
Josephine (*crossly*) No, I'm too hot. *Why* did Hickory and Rekelen have to come up from the other side? Now we must wait for them.
Thomas They wanted to take the kidnappers by surprise, of course.
Josephine *I* don't see any kidnappers! I don't see anybody but us!
Charlotte (*still enchanted with the view*) It's like being on top of the world! —Oh, look—there's a great golden bird down there!
Thomas
Josephine } (*running up*) Where?
Charlotte (*climbing down to the phoenix*) I think it's dead.
Josephine Oh, poor thing.
Thomas It's a very large bird.
Charlotte Perhaps it isn't dead. Lift up its head. Gently. If only we could find some water!

Thomas and Josephine support the Phoenix's head

> *Mrs Noah appears at the top of the mountain followed by Noah. He has a blue cloak draped from his shoulders and wears a long, white beard. In his hand is a coil of rope*

Mrs Noah (*furiously*) They've got my turkey!! (*She hurries down to them*) Just what do you think you're doing? Take your hands off that bird, it's mine!!—Noah, don't stand there like a graven image—tie it up and take it home!
Charlotte Oh, don't tie it up—it may not be dead!
Mrs Noah (*grabbing a wing*) Thieves and robbers!! Release my turkey at once!! Noah, be quick with that rope, the saucepan will boil over before we've got the bird plucked!
Children PLUCKED???
Phoenix (*sitting up suddenly*) PLUCKED???
Mrs Noah Oh, goodness gracious, it's still alive. Noah, you must wring its neck!
Noah (*protesting mildly*) But, my dear . . .
Phoenix (*in an awful voice*) I command you to release me upon the instant! I am the fabulous Phoenix—look upon me and tremble!!
Mrs Noah You're not a turkey then?
Phoenix Do I *look* like a turkey?
Thomas I don't think you do. Not a bit.
Phoenix This is a sensible boy. A boy to be commended. (*To Thomas*) If you can spare the time I will tell you the story of my life!—I am, at the present moment, five hundred years old . . .
Mrs Noah Five hundred years? It might be a bit tough!
Phoenix Yesterday I built my funeral nest of aromatic twigs and branches.
Mrs Noah So *that's* where my firewood went!
Phoenix (*quelling her with a look*) I do this regularly, you understand, every five hundred years. The pattern is always the same. I build the nest, lay the famous golden egg, flap my wings to create the sacred flame,

Act I, Scene 3   19

and am at once consumed by the fire. Then, from the heart of the glowing ashes I am hatched from the egg, and arise once more, ready for another five hundred years.
Mrs Noah Good gracious me, what a performance just to cook an egg!
Phoenix (*annoyed*) Kindly hold your tongue! You are confusing my story. Now, where was I?
Josephine About to be consumed by the fire.
Phoenix Ah, but that is just what I was not! When I flapped my golden wings to create the sacred flame nothing happened! I have lost the power, and what is to become of me now only the prophets know!
Charlotte Don't be sad! I expect it is because time has stopped. Most things are very odd just now.
Noah (*moving towards the Phoenix*) Your story is very interesting. Very interesting indeed. You know, I was under the impression that the Phoenix always built its nest upon the burning desert sands of Arabia.
Phoenix It doesn't necessarily have to be Arabia. I like an occasional change of scene, you know. And the burning desert sands can get very boring.
Noah Naturally, naturally. Why, I find the top of this mountain a little wearisome at times. That's why our children went, you know. They were bored. They travelled south, east and west, and left Mrs Noah and myself alone here.—But that's the way with children.

Noah is about to enlarge on this point when Hickory's voice is heard. He appears at the top of the mountain followed by Rekelen, and straightway launches into impassioned speech

Hickory Stop!! Don't move, any of you—we've got you surrounded!—You devils, you'll pay for this!—Just you wait till I get hold of you! You won't get away with it, you know! We know he's here! We've got our information!—You've put the whole world in jeopardy, you have!—I insist that you release him!—*And* we're not paying any ransom, either!!

He has pushed and scrambled his way through to Noah, and taken his hand

Hickory Don't worry Father Time, you're safe now! We'll have you back home in a jiffy! (*For the first time he looks Noah in the face*) You're *not* him!!
Rekelen I mentioned it as we come over the top. I mentioned that I may have made a mistake. One long white beard, I said, is much like another. And so it appears to be!
Hickory (*very confused*) Then *who* is this?
Rekelen Allow me to introduce you.—Mr Noah, Mr Dock. Mr Dock, Mr Noah.
Noah (*shaking hands with Hickory*) How do you do, Mr Dock? (*Turning to Rekelen*) But, my dear sir, haven't we met before?—Aren't you . . . ?—Didn't I . . . ?
Rekelen Perfectly correct, Mr Noah. You sent me out from the Ark to look for dry land.

Noah So I did!—Yes!—Let me see, that must have been two or three thousand years ago!—Did you find any?
Rekelen Eventually.
Noah Ah, yes. The Dove was quicker—I remember now.
Josephine Has anyone thought what we should do next? If Father Time isn't on this mountain—where is he?
Rekelen *That* is the burning question.
Phoenix Do you mind not mentioning burning? In view of my present situation I find the subject in very poor taste.
Rekelen Then why listen in to a private conversation?
Charlotte Oh, please don't quarrel! We are in such a dreadful position, stuck on the top of this mountain, and not knowing which way to turn.
Rekelen If you ask my advice . . .
Hickory We *did*, and you were wrong!
Phoenix Perhaps it would be better to ask someone with a little more knowledge of the world. I understand you have lost Father Time?
Hickory (*bitterly*) He's been kidnapped.
Phoenix I shouldn't be at all surprised. Describe him!
Hickory Long white beard—*very* long, down to here. White hair, grey eyes, white tunic, blue cloak. Carries a scythe. Never without it.
Thomas And he's about a billion years old.
Phoenix Ah, fairly young!—Well, as it is apparent that my funeral pyre will not burn until time starts again, I had better help you to find him. Be seated all of you, and if you can, be quiet. I need a calm and peaceful atmosphere, so no irritating vibrations, if you please!

The Phoenix pulls a golden feather from behind its ear, and gazes through it

Phoenix (*chanting*) Phoenix, through your feather bright,
                Gaze steadfast into endless night!
                Seek for a beard both long and white!
Rekelen It sounds uncommonly like a fortune-teller.
Everyone Ssh!
Phoenix I see it—I see it! On a green and ferny hillock in the western hemisphere, stands a person with a long white beard, grey eyes and a blue cloak.—Ah, the mists are closing about it. The picture fades!
Rekelen *Exactly* like a fortune-teller!
Hickory It's Father Time, I *know* it is! Can you take us there, Phoenix?
Phoenix (*making a ghastly joke*) You find the time—I'll find the place!
Hickory (*opening the Time Box*) Everyone take a dandelion clock.

They do so

Thomas (*handing one to the Phoenix*) It's a jolly good job there was a spare one!
Hickory (*to the world*) Now, world, are you still there? Well, blow as hard as you can! All together—one—two—three—BLOW!!

The dandelion seeds blow into the air. The great clock ticks slowly, and the children and Rekelen, following Hickory and the Phoenix, are whirled

Act I, Scene 4   21

away. The Time Trogs move the cubes and when the music of time ceases we are in a green, ferny world—a woodland place

Scene 4

THE LAND OF THE GOBLINS

Goblin music is playing in this green world. The kind of music that makes you want to dance more than anything else. Three Goblins come through the glade, these are Gooseberry, Glumm and Goatnose. Glumm and Goatnose are putting up a small wicket gate. Gooseberry is sweeping with a broom made of twigs. He wears a ticket-punching machine

Goatnose (*manouvering his end of the gate*) To you a bit more, Glumm.
Glumm It's all very well you saying that, Goatnose—but it won't go to me any more. It's stuck!
Goatnose Give it a pull. It went all right last year.
Glumm I know it went all right last year, but the grass has grown up since then.
Gooseberry (*who has been leaning on his broom and tapping his feet to the music*) Listen to that, boys! They're tuning up! They're into the swing of it!—When I hear that I could dance for a week!
Glumm You may have to. If King Glinter decides to dance for a week, than everybody dances for a week!
Goatnose (*leaving the gate and coming down to Gooseberry*) Sounds all right, that does, Gooseberry my lad!—I like the Autumn Revels. I like them better than the Summer Revels.
Gooseberry Or the Spring Revels.
Glumm I like the In-Between Revels best.
Gooseberry There aren't any In-Between Revels, Glumm.
Glumm So, I like them best. My feet aren't none too good at dancing.

The dancing music fades and a silvery-sounding horn echoes through the glade

Gooseberry On duty, lads! There's the signal! Look out for a rush!

Gooseberry stations himself at the wicket gate. Glumm and Goatnose line up behind him

Gooseberry Here comes the first lot. It's the red-caps as usual!

A party of red-capped Goblins carrying large admission tickets and laughing and chattering come up to the gate

Gooseberry (*very official, and getting his ticket machine ready*) Tickets please!
1st Red Cap Hello, hello, hello! Here's old Gooseberry! How are things, Gooseberry?

2nd Red Cap Going to be a good do tonight?
3rd Red Cap Not late, are we?
Gooseberry (*punching tickets as fast as he can*) Just in time. Glumm will show you to your places.

Goatnose opens the gate and the red-caps are shown to their places on the cubes by Glumm. They are closely followed in by a crowd of yellow-capped Goblins, all in an exceedingly frivolous mood. The music has started again, and along with their talking and laughing the Goblins clap and stamp their feet in time to it. And every now and then they put their hands to their mouths and emit a strange hissing sound. While Gooseberry is seeing the yellow-caps through the gate, the rescue party, led by the Phoenix, appears at the edge of the clearing

Phoenix This is the place to which the golden feather has led us. There is the hillock on which the white-beard sat.
Hickory I'll see if we can get in while nobody's looking.

Hickory moves forward to the wicket gate which is now closed. Gooseberry, who has been chatting to some friends, turns to look at him. The music has stopped—

Gooseberry (*in a clear and warning voice*) I spy strangers!

All the Goblins become quiet and look towards Hickory

Goblins Strangers? (*They hiss*)
Gooseberry I spy no-beards!
Goblins No-beards? (*They hiss again*)
Gooseberry (*moving to the gate*) Get out! Go back!—No admittance to strangers!
Goblins No admittance! (*The hissing is very loud now*)
Goatnose Ticket holders only, this way!
Goblins Ticket holders only! (*They snigger nastily*)
Glumm Only persons with beards are allowed in!!
Goblins Only beards are beautiful! (*Hiss*)
Hickory I'm sorry to bother you, but could I . . . ?

At this moment the silver trumpet sounds once more and a herald Goblin leaps on to the centre cube

Herald Hear one! Hear all!—His Gobliness King Glinter of this glade invites you all to a draught of clover wine in the Royal Enclosure. To be quaffed before the dancing commences! Come one! Come all!

The trumpet sounds again and the Herald departs. The Goblins knock one another over in their eagerness to follow

Gooseberry (*thumping Glumm on the back*) Look after the gate like a good chap, Glumm! We'll bring you back a draught of wine!

Act I, Scene 4

Gooseberry and Goatnose depart with the rest leaving Glumm on the gate

When the noise of the departing Goblins has died down Hickory tries again

Hickory Could you please . . . ?
Glumm NO!—No tickets, no entry!—No beards, no admittance!
Josephine (*coming up to the gate*) It really is *very* important!
Glumm (*scandalized*) Females?
Josephine Yes, but——
Glumm No females allowed into the glade!

Glumm folds his arms and stands with his back to the gate. Josephine and Hickory go back to the rest of the party

Hickory We *must* get in there somehow. Think of Father Time waiting to be rescued!
Thomas I could climb over the gate when the goblin wasn't looking. Or squeeze through the bars!
Charlotte What use would that be? You couldn't rescue Father Time on your own! You saw how many goblins there are in there, and they don't look particularly friendly.
Phoenix I know these goblin creatures, the one thing they cannot resist is a gift. Some pretty trifle, like the ribbons which bind your hair, and that thick-headed creature at the gate would let you in at once, tickets or no tickets.
Hickory It would be worth trying.
Thomas But what about beards? You heard what they said. Hickory and I would never get in without beards.
Josephine It's a pity we're not at home. We've got beards in the dressing-up box.
Charlotte What about the Parcel Woman? Would she have beards in her cupboard?
Josephine She has most things.
Thomas Rekelen could ask her. Could you go back, Rekelen?
Charlotte How would he get there?
Rekelen (*loftily*) A raven has its own time. A raven moves in the upper streams of air, alert to the winds of change, and . . .
Phoenix (*impatiently*) Your dusty friend talks too much. If he is going, then let him go!—I shall rest meanwhile, I am finding this journey somewhat exhausting!

The Phoenix moves away and roosts. Rekelen flaps his dusty wings, utters a loud "caw" and departs

Hickory It might be a good idea if the rest of us looked around to see if there is another way in.
Thomas (*eager to explore*) Oh yes, let's do that! Come on, Hickory!
Josephine We needn't be away so *very* long.

Charlotte (*who is always thoughtful*) Someone should stay in case Rekelen gets back first.
Thomas Don't worry, the Phoenix is here.
Phoenix (*from its shadowy corner*) The Phoenix is asleep.
Charlotte I don't mind staying if you promise not to be too long. I can wake the Phoenix if anything happens.
Phoenix (*sleepily*) Only in a case of grave emergency.
Charlotte Naturally.
Thomas (*who can hardly wait to go*) Come on, let's go!
Josephine We won't be long, Charley, I promise.
Charlotte (*sitting down with her back to a ferny cube*) I shall be all right.

Hickory, Thomas and Josephine tip-toe away

A moment's silence, only slightly disturbed by the heavy, slumberous breathing of the Phoenix. Glumm, who is still at his post at the gate, looks around and sees no-one

Glumm They've gone. I thought they would. I'll just take the weight off my feet.

Glumm settles down inside the gate. His eyes close almost at once

A rattle of tins, a clanking and a scrabbling, cause Charlotte to sit up straight and open her eyes. Frod appears, balancing precariously on a cube. He calls back into the leafy shadows

Frod (*calling*) I'm there, Harley!—I say, I'm there!!

He waves his arms triumphantly and falls to the ground. Charlotte jumps up and stands looking at the heap of tins in amazement

Frod (*calling from in among the tins*) I'm all right!—Not to worry, Harley, I'm all right!!—I'm not too sure about the condensed milk, but the rest of me is fine!—Help me up, can't you?

Charlotte, a little apprehensively holds out a hand and pulls Frod to his feet. He is looking anxiously at his equipment

Frod Ta. I can't remember, did I have the tin-opener, or didn't I? Because if I did I've lost it! (*He looks up and is very surprised at the sight of Charlotte*) Oh!—Good evening!
Charlotte Good evening.
Frod (*floundering*) Are you?—Did you?—I mean—can you speak English?
Charlotte I am English.
Frod Oh. Are you—a girl?
Charlotte Yes.
Frod Oh. Excuse me. (*He rummages among his gear for a phrase book*) Girls, English. (*He finds the place in his book and, clearing his throat, reads in a loud, self-conscious voice*) "Good evening, miss. Can you show me the way to the Post Office?"

Act I, Scene 4

Charlotte Do you really want to go to the Post Office?
Frod Not much. I say, are you the enemy?
Charlotte I don't think so.
Frod Good. You don't look like it. (*Shyly*) Thank you for helping me up.
Charlotte That's quite all right. Why are you carrying all those tins of food?
Frod I'm not supposed to tell. You see, it's a military secret.
Charlotte Oh. I'm sorry I asked.
Frod That's all right.
Harley's Voice Frod!!—Where are you??—Where you gone and got to, Frod??
Frod (*calling back*) I'm over here, Harley.—It's all right, I only dented the condensed milk!
Harley (*whose head has appeared over the top of the cube*) Never mind the condensed milk!—Get back over this side!—Why don't you follow the compass?
Frod (*climbing up on the cube*) I never had the compass, Harley.
Harley You never had it?
Frod No, Harley.
Harley Then who had the compass?

A Plutonian argument breaks out in the background

Harley Oh, shut up! (*They do*) Frod—get back over here! (*Harley's head disappears*)
Frod Yes, Harley. (*He looks at Charlotte*) I got to go now. Good-bye.
Charlotte Good-bye!

Frod clanks off

Harley's Voice Frod!! Watch the noise!!
Frod Sorry, Harley.

He goes. As Frod clanks away Rekelen appears at Charlotte's side, a parcel under his wing

Rekelen You were speaking to someone?
Charlotte (*who has been gazing after Frod*) What?—Oh, Rekelen, it's you. Yes, I *was* speaking to someone, but I'm not quite sure what kind of person it was. Did you get the beards?
Rekelen I did. And I bring a message from the Parcel Woman. She hears things, you know. She has acquaintances.
Charlotte What is the message?
Rekelen I will tell it to everyone or to no-one!

At this moment the scouting party returns

Charlotte Oh, good! Here are the others. Did you find another way in?
Josephine There isn't one. The place is surrounded by thick thorn bushes. No-one could get through.

Charlotte Rekelen's back.

Thomas (*rushing to the raven*) That was quick. Did you get the beards?

Rekelen I did.

Rekelen hands the parcel to Thomas who opens it, taking out two white beards

Charlotte And he's got a message from the Parcel Woman!

Hickory (*who is putting in his beard*) Tell us.

Rekelen They ask you to be quick, for the whole of mankind is in a ferment! Great ships are stranded in the middle of the oceans. Aeroplanes hang motionless in the sky. In the parliaments of the world men sit in rows like graven images. Father Time *must* be found!

Thomas Don't worry—we'll find him! Give us the hair ribbons, we'd better try our luck!

Hickory If I might make a suggestion, I think the rest of you should keep out of sight. We don't want to antagonize this person at the gate!

Charlotte Take care.

Rekelen and the girls move back into the shadows, as Hickory and Thomas, trying to look as much like goblins as possible, advance towards the gate

Thomas (*in as goblin a voice as he can manage*) Excuse me, sir! Will you open the gate?

Glumm wakes up with a start

Glumm What?—Who's that?—Tickets, please!

Hickory (*also disguising his voice*) I'm afraid we've lost our tickets, sir. Will these do instead?

They hang the girl's bright hair ribbons temptingly in front of Glumm

Glumm (*touching the ribbon with his forefinger*) Beautiful!—Oh yes, beautiful!—Lost your tickets you say?

Hickory Dropped them down a rabbit hole on the way along. *You* know what rabbit holes are like!

Glumm Ah yes. *I* know what rabbit holes are like!

The goblin music starts again, very loudly, and over it the high voices of hundreds of Goblins, laughing and shrieking with delight. In they come in a tremendous dance. Stamping, leaping and hopping in time to the music

Glumm (*opening the gate*) The great dance has started. Quick, you'd better come in. The King will allow no-one in once the dance has begun!

Thomas and Hickory, jostled by the dancing Goblins, move to a position on one of the ferny cubes. They watch, fascinated, as the line of Goblins snakes about, faster and faster. On certain beats the Goblins put their hands to their mouths and make their curious hissing sound

Glumm (*to Hickory and Thomas*) You *must* join in the dance! The King insists that everyone must dance.

Act I, Scene 4

Hickory Which is the King?
Glumm He won't appear until the dancing is at its height. But he watches it. He knows those who dance and those who do not. Come, we must join in!

They join the mass of Goblins who dance faster and faster, their screams and hisses getting louder and louder. When the dance is at its height, a figure with a long white beard and flowing blue cloak appears on the topmost cube. Hickory, who has just completed a most complicated dance step, turns and catches sight of the figure

Hickory (*at the top of his voice*) Father Time!!

Everything stops. The silence is complete—the dancers like figures carved from stone. Slowly the blue-cloaked figure turns on its pinnacle, and the cold, steely eyes of the Goblin King alight on Thomas who has lost his beard in the heat of the dance

King Glinter (*his voice like ice*) I spy strangers!
Goblins Strangers! (*They hiss*)
King Glinter I spy a no-beard!
Goblins No-beard! (*Hiss*)
King Glinter Seize him!
Goblins Seize him!

Hissing loudly the Goblins surround Thomas and hustle him towards the King

King Glinter Cut off his ears!
Goblins (*stamping and hissing*) Cut off his ears!
Glinter Pull out his hair!
Goblins Pull out his hair!

The Goblins are working themselves into a frenzy, and after Thomas's blood! Hickory, who has managed to get out of the crush and over to the gate, blows a great blast on his whistle

Hickory (*calling to Thomas*) It's not him! It's not Father Time!—But don't worry, Thomas, I'll save you!!

Hickory goes into his mouse-frightening routine. The Goblins, like the Mice, are mesmerized by its awfulness. They stand, eyes wide and mouths agape. At the final whistle blast they flee, screaming

Hickory Run Thomas! RUN!!!

Thomas does run—towards the gate. They are through it just as the moon drops from the sky, and a grey darkness overwhelms them

Thomas It worked, didn't it, Hickory?
Hickory Yes, it did. It's a good little routine, that!—And now, Thomas, we must find the others.

END OF ACT I

ACT II

Scene 1

THE LAND OF LIMBO

The gate and the Goblins are gone. The ferny, leafy cubes are still there, but bathed in a grey light. Rekelen and the Phoenix are roosting. Hickory and the three children sit sadly on the cubes

Hickory As soon as he turned round I knew it wasn't Father Time. But from the back he looked *exactly* like him.
Josephine What are we going to do? It's no use blowing the dandelion clocks if we don't know where to go.
Charlotte I hate this place, it's so grey and silent. I suppose if no-one comes we shall be here forever.
Josephine We can go back to the clock. There's enough dandelion time left to take us there.
Hickory (*fiercely*) I *won't* go back without Father Time! I will *not* give up!—If he's not in the clock then he's somewhere else, and I shall find him!—Of course, you can go back if you like! I expect I can manage on my own.
Charlotte Of course we won't go back, Hickory. We want to help.
Thomas That's right. *I* don't want to live in a world where time has stopped and I have to wear these stupid clothes!
Josephine Shall we ask the Phoenix to try again?
Thomas No thank you!—Look what happened last time! Why, those goblins were going to cut off my ears!
Phoenix (*sleepily, from the corner*) Anyone can make a mistake.
Charlotte (*who has moved away from the others*) I do believe someone is coming. Listen!—Isn't that a voice?

There does seem to be a voice somewhere in the shadows. The rescue party stand together, peering into the gloom

> *Out of the gloom come the muffled cries of sea-birds, and a woman's voice soothing them. It is the Goose Woman. She carries a sack over her shoulders. She sits on a cube and opens the mouth of the sack*

Goose Woman Come along now, quietly—quietly. I know the air is still, but you *shall* fly again, my beauties. You *shall* fly again.
Josephine Who can it be?
Rekelen (*coming forward*) The Goose Woman, I believe. (*He goes to her*) Is that you, Goose Woman? What have you in the sack?

Goose Woman Eh?—Is it Rekelen, the old raven?—My eyes are not too steady in this limbo-light.
Rekelen It is.
Goose Woman Good gracious, how you haven't changed! As dusty as ever, I see. Are you caught as well, Rekelen? I should have thought you too wily an old bird. These in my sack were trapped in the under-tow of time. Skuas and black-backs. The world is in a bewilderment. Have you any news of the trouble?
Rekelen Father Time has been taken from the clock labyrinth, Goose Woman. We are searching for him. Have you, in your wanderings, seen him?
Goose Woman Is that the trouble?—Describe.
Hickory Long beard, grey eyes, long blue cloak.
Goose Woman When I saved these who are in my sack, there was a person such as you say, seated on a wild rock in the Middle Ocean. The sun glinted on something that he held in his hand.
Hickory (*excitedly*) The scythe! He always carries a scythe! It's Father Time, I know it is!
Goose Woman That may be. *I* thought it was a graven image!
Hickory Can you show us the way, Goose Woman?—We have some Dandelion Time left in the box.
Goose Woman Not I. There are geese to pluck for the winter. Ask Rekelen. He knows the Middle Ocean.
Rekelen Like the back of my wing.
Hickory (*opening the Time Box*) Then take the dandelion clocks and let us move on.
Phoenix I trust the Middle Ocean will not make my feathers too damp. This could have serious consequences when I am about to be consumed in the flames of my funeral pyre!
Rekelen A selfish attitude if I may say so!
Charlotte SSh!
Hickory (*coming forward*) Are you there world? And are you ready? Now we must move to a rock in the Middle Ocean. Blow well, and blow hard! One, two, three, BLOW!!

Everyone blows very hard, but time does not move

Josephine Nothing's happening!
Rekelen It may be that the world is not blowing hard enough!
Phoenix Possibly it has lost interest.
Goose Woman Possibly. It is well known that the world is quick to lose interest in a difficult situation. It becomes bored.—It prefers to sit in rows, watching and doing nothing!
Hickory (*to the world*) Oh, world, don't lose interest now!—You'll regret it if you do! Shall we try once more? Are you ready?—One, two, three, BLOW!!

They all blow as hard as they can, but still nothing happens

Charlotte How *awful!*—Are we stuck here forever?

Josephine (*bursting into tears*) Oh, Charley, I'm frightened! I want to go home!

Charlotte and Thomas move to Josephine and put their arms round her

Charlotte Don't cry, Jo.
Thomas Think of poor Father Time stuck on a rock in the Middle Ocean!
Josephine Oh, why did he want to go and get himself kidnapped?
Phoenix My sentiments exactly. It was extremely careless of him.
Hickory Well, I *told* you you can go back, and so you can!—*I'm* not keeping you here! Don't bother about me!
Josephine But we're not able to go back—the Dandelion clocks won't blow!
Goose Woman There is an answer here somewhere. I can hear it in the air. Listen!

They all listen. From the shadows a voice is talking happily to itself. It seems to be saying a kind of table

North Wind "Two puffs are one blow,
 Three blows are one blast,
 Four blasts are one gale,
 Five gales are one storm,
 Six storms are one tempest."
No. That ain't right. "Six storms are one hurricane, Seven hurricanes are one tempest."
Goose Woman I thought so! I *thought* so!!—

She steps up to a cube and roughly pulls the North Wind from behind it. He carries a sack which he is tying tightly at the neck

North Wind Ow! Ouch!! Let go of me!!
Goose Woman It's the North Wind, that's who it is. He's the cause of all the trouble.
North Wind (*squirming in her grasp*) No I ain't, Goose Woman. I ain't the cause of nothing!—Ouch!—let go of me!
Goose Woman (*releasing him*) What have you in the sack, young Nor'?
North Wind (*rubbing his ear*) Nothing. I ain't got nothing in the sack.
Goose Woman I'll ask you again, and this time I'll have a proper answer. What have you in the sack?
North Wind (*after thinking for a moment*) Chickens.
Goose Woman Don't lie to me, young Nor'! I know a sack of chickens when I see one! (*She grabs his ear again*) The breath of the world is in that sack!—You have been stealing it to save yourself the trouble of blowing!—You've stolen the breath of the world!
North Wind (*indignantly*) No, I never have!
Goose Woman Lies, as well, young Nor'?
North Wind I was just sitting back there having a rest and learning my tables, when the world's breath suddenly blew into my sack!

Act II, Scene 2   31

Goose Woman And tied itself in with a stout cord!—How convenient! Well, watch that it blows out again when the word is given, or I'll have you lashed to a rock in the burning desert wastes, for a hundred years or more!
North Wind (*terrified*) Oh, don't do that, Goose Woman! I couldn't never abide all that heat!—I'll undo the cord when the word is given!
Goose Woman *And* blow hard yourself, into the bargain!
North Wind I'll blow to the strength of a snow storm, Goose Woman!
Goose Woman That's more like it! (*To Hickory*) Give the word!
Hickory Are you all ready? One, two, three, BLOW!!

The World blows. Everyone in Limbo blows, and the North Wind releases the breath from his sack, creating a biting blast of snow-laden wind. The great clock ticks. The music of time begins, and the rescue party are whirled away as the Time Trogs move the cubes

SCENE 2

BENEATH THE OCEAN

A rippling green sea is washing over the high rocks. Various sea creatures are moving busily about on the sea bed. Crabs, lobsters, star fish etc., Sea Maidens lie about on the rocks combing their long hair

Three Drowned Sailors come through the rocks. They each carry a bucket, and they dance along the bed of the ocean singing

All the Sea-People join in the chorus and in the Sailors' dance. The Sailors sing their song to the tune of "What shall we do with the drunken sailor?"

Sailors (*singing*)
    What shall we do with the brown sea-lettuce?
    Fresh and crisp and quite as wet as
    An octopus caught in a fisherman's net is,
    Early in the morning!
        Chorus:
    Hooray and up we rises
    Catching crabs in various sizes,
    Rescuing fish before they fry-ses,
    Early in the morning!
    Here is a bucket of poor old winkles,
    Shells gone dry and covered in wrinkles,
    Waiting for the sea to smooth their crinkles,
    Early in the morning!
        Chorus:
    Hooray we all assemble,
    Up on the beach where the jelly-fish tremble,
    Like the prunes they so resemble,
    Early in the morning!

Where shall we put these "dead-men's fingers"?
All provided with poison stingers?
Oh, how the smell of the sea-weed lingers,
Early in the morning!
>> *Chorus:*
Hooray and up we're going,
Where the salty breeze is blowing,
And the tide's no longer flowing
Early in the morning!

The dance is at its height when Thetis comes through the rocks

Thetis I *was* trying to have my afternoon nap, but that seems to be impossible with all the noise that's going on out here! No-one would think that this was the palace of the King of the Oceans! (*She looks at the three Drowned Sailors*) And *what* have you in those nasty buckets?

1st Drowned Sailor Why, bless your heart, Your Royal Highness, ma'am—'tes the "rescuing"!

Thetis The "rescuing"?

2nd Drowned Sailor The rescuing of all them poor creatures what is stranded 'igh and dry on the beaches, ma'am.

3rd Drowned Sailor On account, ma'am, of there not being no tides no more. And they being stuck at 'igh water mark, so to speak!

Thetis I know all about the rescue operation, but why are these creatures being brought here?

1st Drowned Sailor On account of His Royal Majesty King Neptune a-telling of us to bring 'em 'ere, ma'am.

2nd Drowned Sailor "Davy," 'e says. "Take 'em to my daughter Thetis" 'e says. "She'll look arter all these creatures," 'e says. "She 'as a 'eart o' gold, she 'as," 'e says.

3rd Drowned Sailor That's wot 'e says!

Thetis Highmindedness is all very well, but these creatures clutter the place up so!—And they smell rather, don't they?

1st Sea Maiden Oh, they *do*, madam. Isn't it *awful*?

Thetis Very unpleasant.

2nd Sea Maiden (*sneezing violently*) It's bringing on my allergy again, madam!

Thetis (*flapping her handkerchief*) Can't you sprinkle something about?

3rd Sea Maiden We *have*, madam. We've used nearly all of your bottle of "Plankton Number Five".

Thetis Oh? Well, it doesn't seem to have made much difference. (*Advancing towards the sailors*) And what are in the buckets?

1st Drowned Sailor There's winkles, ma'am.

2nd Drowned Sailor And "Dead men's Fingers", ma'am.

3rd Drowned Sailor And a load of sea-worms, ma'am.

The Sea Maidens shriek in horror

Thetis They must all go down into the locker. I can't do with them up here. Where *is* King Neptune?

Act II, Scene 2   33

1st Drowned Sailor 'Is Royal Majesty is up the Inchcape Rock, ma'am.
3rd Drowned Sailor A-ringing of the bell, and a-rescuing of the larger creatures, ma'am.
Thetis (*very apprehensively*) The *larger* creatures?
2nd Drowned Sailor That's right, ma'am. "Davy," 'e says, "you three go on with the buckets full," 'e says, "while I stays 'ere," 'e says, "and rescues the whales and sharks and stuff," 'e says.
3rd Drowned Sailor That's wot 'e says.
Thetis *Whales* and *sharks*?
1st Drowned Sailor And sea-cows, ma'am.
Thetis (*stamping her foot*) I will *not* have great fat sea-cows in my nice clean palace!

With a great fuss and chattering a crowd of young Sea Cucumbers push on from the direction of the shore

Sea Cucumbers Don't shove—I never did—you're pushing—look at my tentacles—I didn't—all in a tangle—I *won't* be first—yes, you must—I'd rather be at the back—don't squash me—etc.
Thetis *What* are *these*?
1st Drowned Sailor More poor unfortunates, ma'am.
2nd Drowned Sailor Wot is being rescued from the tide-less shores, ma'am.
3rd Drowned Sailor And brought 'ere to you for safe-keeping, ma'am.
Thetis But what *are* they?
1st Drowned Sailor Sea cucumbers, ma'am.
Thetis Oh. Can you eat them?

There is a shocked silence. The little Sea Cucumbers look at Thetis and turn pale. The Sea Cucumber's song is sung to the tune of "Yes, we have no bananas"

Sea Cucumbers (*singing*)
  You can't eat a cucumber,
  When a cucumber comes from the sea!
  There's cucumbers what grow just for salad, I know!
  You eat them with lettuce and onions, but oh,
  You can't eat a cucumber,
  When a cucumber comes from the sea!
Thetis (*putting her hand to her head*) I really cannot do with all this noise!—Davy, take them away to the locker.
2nd Drowned Sailor Ay, ay, ma'am!—Sea cucumbers, right turn! By the left, quick march!

The three Drowned Sailors march the line of Sea Cucumbers off to the locker

Thetis (*clapping her hands*) Come, maidens, to my coral bower, and brush my hair!—I *must* get rid of this headache before King Neptune comes home. He has such a *very* loud voice.
Sea Maidens Yes, madam.

Thetis (*as she goes*) Did you say you had used *all* my Plankton Number Five?

Thetis and the Sea Maidens retire to the bower. For a moment the sea bed is empty, and then, to the strains of the Plutonian battle cry, Harley marches in his Picked Body of Men. They wear, in addition to their tweed caps, underwater goggles and flippers

Plutonians One two, left right,
     Clap three, stamp four!
     We are from Pluto!
     Left right, clap five!
Harley Company, halt!!

They do so

Harley Fall out for refreshments!

The Picked Body of Men sit down thankfully on the rocks. Harley goes to a rock at the back and communes with a two-way radio

Till What about a drink then, Frod?
Frod What about a what?
Tull What about a drink?
Frod Where you going to get a drink then?
Dred You're going to give us one.
Frod I am?
Binjer Look, stupid, you got them hanging round your neck, haven't you?
Frod That's right, so I have. What do you want?
Binjer What you got?
Frod (*looking at his tins*) I got orange juice, I got tomato soup, I got condensed milk—oh no, I squashed that one. I got . . .
Dred Have you got the tin-opener?
Frod Harley says I never had the tin-opener.
Till Binjer had the tin-opener.
Binjer That's right, I had the tin-opener.
Dred Well, hand it over. I fancies the tomato soup.
Frod (*slowly reading the label*) "Tomato soup. Heat—in—a—saucepan—over—a—low—flame."—Who had the little primus stove?
Binjer Till had the little primus stove.
Till I still got the little primus stove!—Who had the matches?

They look at one another in dismay

Binjer We never got given no matches.
Dred I know *I* never got given none!
Frod So far as what I know, nobody got given none.
Till (*fed up*) That's nice, that is. In't it nice? I takes care of the little primus stove, but so far as we know nobody got given no matches!

Harley comes back

Act II, Scene 2   35

Harley All right, you lot. On your feet!
Till But, Harley ...
Harley You can't sit about here all day, stuffing yourselves and guzzling what Frod's got in his tins!
Dred But, Harley ...
Harley I've got my duty to do!
Binjer But, Harley ...
Harley *Someone* has got to run this campaign!
Frod But, Harley ...
Harley (*furiously*) Shut up, Frod!!—You never stop, do you? You're always on about something!
Frod Sorry, Harley.
Harley I have just been in touch with Base. The King, His Royal Majesty King Billiam the Tenth, is very pleased with the way what the kidnapping of a certain Earth person went off. The kidnapped person is now safe in the Plutonian Jail, and is being closely studied by Plutonian scientists.
Frod Who is, Harley?
Harley The prisoner.
Binjer Why?
Harley To see what he does to make his beard grow, stupid!
Dred I don't do nothing to make my beard grow. Do you do anything to make your beard grow, Till?
Till No, I don't do nothing.
Harley (*exasperated*) That is because you are not able to grow beards, you 'orrible little Plutonians, you!—Nobody on Pluto can grow a beard, which is why we've captured this Earth person who *can* grow a beard, to find out how he does it!
Dred Why?
Harley Because the King of Pluto wants to grow a beard, that's why!! Now, shut up and listen!! I've been given, by Base, a description of the rescue party wot's trying to find the Earth person, and get him back. Our job is to prevent that rescue party from finding him. Their description is as follows. Two large birds, one yellow, one black. Two girls with long hair. One boy, and one clock person. Anyone seeing that lot reports to me at once—is that clear?
Frod I seen a girl, once.
Dred You never!
Frod Yes, I did. She had long hair. She was nice. I spoke to her.
Binjer What did you say?
Frod I said "Good evening, miss, can you show me the way to the Post Office?"
Till You never!
Frod I *did*!
Harley (*working himself up into a rage*) I've warned you, Frod!—I've warned you, over and over again, I have warned you ...!

Harley is just getting into his stride, and Frod is trembling so that all his tins rattle together, when a terrible roar, like the voice of a wounded sea-bull, sounds from above. On the top of the topmost rock stands Father Neptune, his face red with anger. He descends to the sea bed in transports of rage

Neptune (*roaring*) Avast and belay!!—What parasites are polluting me palace??—What earth-bound bodies are bubbling about among me barnacles?—I'll have you know that I am the King of all the Oceans!!—Neptune is me name, and nasty me nature!!—I'll shred you into shavings and shovel you to the sharks!—I'll wallop you with a whale's fin!!!—You can't scuffle up me sea bed and get off scot free!!—Where's me daughter???—Where's me drowned sailors?—Where's everybody???

Harley (*quietly to his squad*) Plutonians, draw aerosols!

They each take an aerosol can from their belt

Neptune (*storming about among the rocks*) Why doesn't somebody come?? (*Bellowing*) Davy Jones!!—Are ye there??
Harley Remove caps!
Neptune (*his voice echoing around the ocean*) Davy Jones!! Where are ye??

The Plutonians remove the caps from their aerosols

Binjer Do we stun 'em or kill 'em, Harley?
Harley We stuns 'em, Binjer. We don't want no trouble as to leaving bodies lying around the ocean.

The three Drowned Sailors rush on with cutlasses drawn. They are followed by Thetis and the Sea Maidens who utter shrieks of dismay

Neptune There you are, me brave lads!—Engage the enemy!!

The Sailors are about to do so, when Harley gives his command

Harley Hold your fire, lads!!—Try 'em with fisticuffs first!!

With blood-curdling yells the Drowned Sailors and the Plutonians engage in hand-to-hand fighting. The Sailors are supported by the Sea Cucumbers who rush on and harass the Plutonians. Harley gives the command to fire. The Plutonians squirt their aerosols at the enemy, and Neptune, Thetis, Sailors, etc., sink to their knees, transfixed

Harley Good shooting, lads. And now, we'll slide silently away to the shore!

They slide silently away. All except Frod, who clanks

Harley (*calling back to him*) Frod—!!
Frod I know, Harley, I know!—"Watch the noise!"

Frod clanks off. The sea bed is silent. Not even a fish swims by. Presently the heads of the rescue party appear over the top rocks. They gaze down into the depths of the ocean

Act II, Scene 2

Thomas Can you see anything, Hickory?
Hickory Not very much.
Charlotte Don't the rocks look odd?
Josephine Yes, they do. Such curious shapes.
Rekelen Those are not rocks but graven images. And I perceive that one of them is wearing a blue cloak, and has a long, white beard.
Josephine So it has. That one, just there! (*She points down at Father Neptune*)
Hickory (*wildly*) Where?—Where??—Show me!!
Charlotte (*pointing down through the sea*) Just there!
Hickory It's him!—It's Father Time! (*Calling*) Father Time, can you hear me?—It's Hickory, come to rescue you from the briny deep!!—Oh, how can I make him look at me? *How* can I make him understand?
Thomas Hang a bit of rope down, and tickle the top of his head with it!
Hickory We haven't any rope!
Josephine Your belt might do, Hickory, if it's long enough.
Hickory (*taking off his belt*) Yes, it might. Now, hold on to me while I let it down.
Phoenix (*edging away*) *Please* don't splash!

Thomas and the girls hold on to Hickory as he reaches down and tries to touch the top of Neptune's head with the belt. After a few goes he is successful. This has the effect of waking Neptune from his trance. He leaps to his feet, shaking his trident at them

Neptune (*his voice roaring through the water*) Avast, and Belay!!
Hickory (*disappointed once again*) Oh, it's not him!!
Neptune (*dancing about with rage*) Who is it who dares to fish with a line for the King of all the Oceans? I'll crush his miserable carcass inside a giant clam!!—I'll tether him with tong-weed and cover him with crabs!! I'll load him with limpets and scatter him with sea-scorpions!!! I'll—I'll ...!!!
Phoenix Shall we go, do you think? A great deal of splashing is taking place!
Charlotte But where *are* we to go?
Phoenix Anywhere is better than here, I should think!
Neptune (*scattering fish left and right as he shakes his trident*) Davy Jones, d'ye hear me???—Drag the villains down to the bottom by their boots, and release the killer whale!!!
Rekelen For once our golden friend is right. The moment to go has now come. Quickly!!

Hickory gives them each a dandelion

Hickory Are you there world?—Blow as hard as you can—we *must* get away from here!! One, two, three, BLOW!!

The clock ticks and they are whisked away. The ocean becomes dark green and Neptune's voice fades into the music of time. The Time Trogs move the cubes into a semi-circle

Scene 3

THE CIRCUS

A Blue Light streams downwards into the half-circle of cubes. The Rescue Party moves in from the shadows to gaze at it

Hickory I wonder what place this is?
Rekelen It was most unfortunate that we were forced to move on without knowing where we wanted to go.
Phoenix At least it is dry here.
Thomas (*who has been examining the designs painted on the cubes*) This is a circus ring. We went to a circus once, and it was exactly like this.
Josephine Thomas is right. And look, the floor has got sawdust on it.
Charlotte (*leaning over a cube and picking something up from the floor of the ring*) A piece of tinsel!—Yes, it must be a circus ring. I expect this came from one of the costumes.

Three Women have entered the circus ring. They carry brooms, and wear tawdry, tattered remnants of circus clothes, covered by coarse aprons and old shawls. Their grey hair hangs untidily about their shoulders. One of them wears a dark shade over her eyes

1st Woman (*crossing to Charlotte*) I'll have that, if you please. (*She takes the piece of tinsel from Charlotte's hand*)
Charlotte (*startled*) Oh, I'm sorry. Is it yours?
1st Woman In a manner of speaking—yes.
Charlotte It was lying there, and I just picked it up.
2nd Woman Quite right. We must keep the ring clear. Nothing should be left to chance.
3rd Woman A piece of tinsel like that could upset the animals.
1st Woman Catch in the toe of a slipper and tangle with the high wire.
2nd Woman Startle a horse, and throw the rider. (*She moves to the side of the ring, covering her face with her hands*)
3rd Woman (*going to her*) Ah, now, Rosie—don't mind!
2nd Woman I don't mind—much.
1st Woman It's a long time ago, Rosie. It's all over now.
3rd Woman You'll be in the ring again, Rosie. Your leg is nearly better. They might send for you next week.
2nd Woman (*bitterly*) Or next month. Or next year.
1st Woman They'll want us all back before long. Performers ain't what they was.
3rd Woman That's true.

The Three Women begin to sweep the ring

Josephine So this *was* a circus.
1st Woman Best in Europe.
3rd Woman Greatest Show On Earth!—That's how they used to bill us!

Act II, Scene 3   39

2nd Woman Packed out every night. Rows and rows of them.
1st Woman Laughing.
2nd Woman And clapping.
3rd Woman And cheering!
1st Woman Rosie here, was the best bare-back rider in the business. Then one night her horse threw her. It was startled by something in the ring.
3rd Woman Could have been a piece of tinsel.
1st Woman Could have.
2nd Woman I've never rode again. And Esther, she've never climbed.
3rd Woman I was a trapeze artiste. One of the Three Silver Miracles. But something went wrong with my eyes. You need good eyes for the trapeze.
1st Woman You got to be able to see in a wink of time. You was good, Esther.
3rd Woman I was.
1st Woman Beautiful she looked, up there on the high wire!—The lights picking sparks from the tinsel on her costume.
Charlotte (*to the first woman*) What were you?
1st Woman Me?—I was the Fat Lady. Only I got too thin! (*She throws back her head and laughs heartily*) Can't have a thin Fat Lady in a circus, can you, young feller-me-lad?
Thomas I wish we could see some of it. Just for a moment.
1st Woman Nothing easier. You only got to think about something, and before you know where you are, it's happening!
2nd Woman Nothing easier. Think about the opening. Think about the Grand Parade, where all the performers come on and march round the ring.
3rd Woman Think about the lights, the music, and the sawdust all smooth and yellow!—Think about the Ringmaster in his top hat!—Think about the clowns!—Why, there's nothing easier!!

On come the great Yellow Lights. Up wells the familiar, brassy, circus music. Into the ring comes the Ringmaster, followed by the Clowns who are tumbling all over the place

Ringmaster Ladies and Gentlemen!!—Welcome to THE GREATEST SHOW ON EARTH!!!!!

The ring is now filled with Circus People marching round to the music. The Three Women shoulder their brooms and join in the grand parade. The Clowns are here, there, and everywhere, with their water-pistols and their custard pies. Charlotte, Josephine and Thomas sit on the side of the ring and cheer and clap! Suddenly Hickory notices, across the other side of the ring, a figure in a long blue cloak

Hickory (*leaping up on to the side of the ring*) It's him! It's Father Time!!
There is a sudden awesome silence as the Circus People turn to look at them

1st Woman *Who* did you say it was?
Hickory (*perhaps not* quite *so certain now*) Father Time.
2nd Woman That's a laugh, that is!—Throw back your hood, Bertha!

The blue-cloaked figure turns and moves into the centre of the ring. She throws back the hood revealing a blonde beard and blonde curls tumbling to her shoulders

3rd Woman He thinks you're Father Time, Bertha!
Bertha Father Time, eh?—Why I'm the biggest attraction in the circus. Haven't you never heard of Bertha the Bearded Lady?
Thomas Is it a real beard?
Bertha D'you hear that?—The kid's asking if it's a real beard!—What a cheek!—'Course it's real. D'you want to try pulling it off?
Thomas (*moving back a bit*) No thank you.

The Circus People laugh, and begin moving away. The Yellow Lights go out. The music fades to a whisper. Only the Blue Light remains, shining on the ring

Thomas Why are they all going?
1st Woman Your friend broke the spell, duck.
2nd Woman Easy to do.
3rd Woman Nothing easier.

The Women move away into the shadows and the ring is deserted once more. Charlotte moves into the centre

Charlotte But, that's the answer really, isn't it? Just like she said. If you think about something hard enough you can make it happen. We've been chasing after people who *look* like Father Time, when what we should do is ask to be taken to where the *real* Father Time is!
Josephine I think you're right, Charley. But how do we do it?
Charlotte Do you remember the very first time we blew the dandelion clocks? Just as the clock began to tick Hickory called out, *very* loudly, "To the mountain!"
Thomas I remember!—And we got to the mountain, didn't we?
Charlotte Yes. Well, this time, when the clock begins to tick, Hickory must call out, "Take us to the real Father Time!"
Josephine We must be sure it'll work because there aren't many seeds left on the dandelion clocks.
Charlotte We can't be sure. But can you think of anything better?
Josephine No, I can't.
Hickory Then we must try it. (*Hickory hands out the dandelion clocks*)

They stand in the centre of the ring. Hickory moves forward

Hickory This may be our last chance, world! So blow as hard as you can! —One, two, three, BLOW!

Act II, Scene 4

The clock begins to tick

Hickory (*shouting above the sound of the clock*) Take us, please, to where the *real* Father Time is!!

They are whirled away as the music swells up and the Time Trogs move the cubes

SCENE 4

THE PLANET PLUTO

*A court room that looks as though it had been carved out of a great cave made of silver and ice. Long spiky icicles hang from the roof. King Billiam and Queen Glary sit on either side of the Judge. The dock and witness box are empty. But the public seats are filled with chattering Plutonians
The Clerk of the Court is at his desk beneath the Judge's seat. The Intercessor is pacing about the court room*

Clerk of the Court (*banging on his desk with a large lump of silver rock* Ho! Ho! Ho!—This court is now in session!—Silence please!— SILENCE!!

The Plutonian public hush one another like anything

Clerk of the Court Ho! Ho! Ho!—In the presence of His Greatness the High Judge of Pluto and their Gracious Majesties King Billiam and Queen Glary, I now declare these proceedings . . .
Intercessor Get on with it.
Clerk I beg your pardon?
Intercessor (*very irritably*) Get on with it!
Clerk Certainly, my lord. Ho! Ho! Ho!
King (*standing up and shouting*) Cut out all that stuff! We know all about that!—Get on with it!
Queen (*also standing up and shouting*) Yes, get on with it, do! Get to the interesting part!
The Public That's right, let's get to the interesting part!
Judge (*leaning forward and speaking to the Clerk*) Perhaps we'd better. It takes time, you know, all that "ho! ho! ho-ing". Call the first witness!
Intercessor First witness!
Clerk First witness!

A small Plutonian Jailor appears in the witness stand, accompanied by his Mother

Judge And who is this?
Intercessor This my lord, is one of the Plutonian jailors.
Judge Ah. Where are the others?
Jailor What others?

Judge The other jailors?
Jailor There ain't any others.
Judge Then why did you mention them?
Jailor I never.
Judge Ah. And who is that in the witness box with you?
Jailor That's my mother.
Judge Your mother?
Jailor That's right.
Judge She'll have to go!
Jailor Why?
Judge Because you can't have your mother in the witness box with you!—Now let's get on!
Clerk Ho! Ho! ho!
Jailor (*to the Clerk*) Oh, shut up!—(*Turning to the Judge*) You can't turn my mum out of the witness box like that!
Public That's quite right—you can't turn her out—etc.,
Jailor My mum goes everywhere with me! Don't you, Mum?

The Jailor's Mother nods vigorously

Jailor She carries my sandwiches, don't you Mum?

She nods again

Jailor I never go nowhere without her. And she never goes nowhere without me.
Judge Well she'll have to go from the witness box.
Jailor If she goes, I go!
Public Quite right too—don't you have it—putting on innocent people etc., etc.
Clerk Silence in court!
Intercessor My lord, *is* this case going to proceed or is it not?
Judge Not with that woman in the witness box.
Jailor Like I said—if she goes—*I* go.
King Oh, let him go!—We've seen him, what more do we want from him?
Judge Your majesty, he must bear witness to the fact that there is a prisoner in the Plutonian jail, and that prisoner, an Earth person.
Queen Then let him do it quickly and then step down.
Judge *Not* with his mother in the witness box with him!
Intercessor If it would help matters along, your lordship, perhaps I should mention that there is another witness ready to swear to the same fact.
Judge (*angrily*) Why didn't you say so before?—First witness dismissed!—Bring on the second witness!
Clerk First witness dismissed!

The Jailor steps down. His Mother stays where she is

Clerk Bring in the second witness!
Judge Just a moment—just a moment!—That woman is still there!
Jailor (*stepping forward*) She won't go unless you tell her to go. Mum only does what she's told—don't you, Mum?

Act II, Scene 4   43

His Mother nods, smiling

Intercessor I think, my lord, if you don't mind my saying so, you'd better tell her to step down.
Judge (*annoyed*) Oh—very well!—First witness's mother, step down!

She steps down. The Jailor comes forward

Jailor Thank you, my lord. This will be the high spot of Mum's life, this will.
Judge Get out!

The Jailor and his Mother depart amid cheers from the public seats

Clerk Second witness!

Harley appears in the stand

King And who is this?
Queen (*frowning*) Whoever he is he had better remove his cap!

Harley takes his cap off

Intercessor Tell his lordship who you are.
Harley I am Harley, your lordship. Leader of the Second Earth Expeditionary Force. Just recalled from active service on that planet, to testify and witness to the fact that the prisoner at present in the Plutonian jail is an Earth person.
Intercessor There are four other witnesses to testify the same!
Judge Bring them to the stand!
Clerk Bring on the other witnesses!

Till, Dred, Binjer and Frod appear beside Harley

Queen (*severely*) They had better remove their caps!

Sheepishly they do so

Judge Do you solemnly swear and testify that the prisoner standing before you in the dock is an Earth person?

They gaze at the dock with their mouths open

King Why don't they answer the question? They are standing there like a lot of graven images!
Queen They had *better* answer! Oh yes, they had *better* answer!
Judge You must answer the question, you know.
Binjer But, your greatness, we can't see no prisoner in the dock!
Queen (*in an awful voice*) No *prisoner*?
King He's quite right, there *is* no prisoner in the dock!—Bring him in at once!—What's the use of a trial without a prisoner?
Judge Call the prisoner!

Clerk Call the prisoner!
Public That's right, bring him on—you can't have a trial without a prisoner—they don't—he isn't—what's the Judge thinking about?—etc., etc.

The Jailor's Mother appears and whispers to the Intercessor

Intercessor Your Lordship, the jailor's mother says that the prisoner is having his dinner.
Queen Having his *dinner*?
Judge His *dinner*?
Public *Having his dinner?*
Intercessor (*having listened to the Jailor's Mother again*) Yes, my Lord, she says he is having tripe and onions.
King Tripe?
Queen And *onions*?
Intercessor Yes, tripe and onions, my Lord!
Public Tripe and onions!—Well, that's better than nothing—I don't like it myself—takes all sorts you know—exactly what I say etc., etc.
Clerk Silence in court!
Queen (*standing up*) I wish to speak.
Clerk Her Majesty wishes to speak!
Judge (*to the clerk*) I'm not deaf, you know. Well, your Majesty?
Queen *What* is a prisoner doing having his dinner in the middle of a trial?—*I'm* not having my dinner!—The King is not having *his* dinner!—*We* are here listening to these ridiculous and badly run proceedings, while the prisoner is eating tripe and onions!—It won't do!—*It will not do!!* He should be hung in chains and starved to death! That's what he should be—*starved to death!!*
King Yes, and then his beard would drop off all right, if he was starved to death! And *I* could wear it! I should be the first King of Pluto to have a beard! (*Working himself up*) I want that beard *now!*—Bring in the prisoner and cut off his beard! I want it *now!!*
Judge But, your Majesty, the scientists say that if you cut off his beard it will fall to pieces.
King (*stamping his foot*) I don't believe it!!—It *won't* fall to pieces!—It *won't!*
Queen (*angrily*) It had better *not* fall to pieces!

The Jailor and his Mother enter, leading the rescue party

Judge What is the meaning of this interruption?
Jailor Begging your Lordship's pardon, but these here persons arrived very sudden like just outside the court-room. So I rounded 'em up and brought 'em in.
Judge Place them in the Dock.

The Jailor and his Mother hustle the rescue party into the dock

Act II, Scene 4

Phoenix I demand instant and unconditional release from this place. I am the famed and fabulous Phoenix. Terrible things will befall any person incarcerating the Phoenix!
Queen (*enchanted*) A talking bird!—What an extraordinary thing!—And golden, too. Could one eat it, I wonder? But perhaps that would be a pity. It might look quite well in a cage, don't you think, Billiam?
Phoenix (*furious beyond anything*) Madam, the wrath of the God of Fire will fall upon your head, if you so much as lift a finger to touch me!
Judge Throw the new prisoners into the dungeons!
Charlotte Oh, don't do that, please!
Frod (*who has recognized her*) No, don't do that!
Charlotte We come from Earth on a very important mission.
Frod That's where I met her. She'll tell you the way to the Post Office if you ask her!
Clerk Silence in Court!
Hickory We believe that Father Time is here on your planet, and we must take him back or the whole of Earth will be plunged into disaster!
Judge Father Time?—Who is this person? Describe him!
Hickory Blue cloak, white tunic, long white beard ...
King That's it—they're after the beard! I *knew* they were! They can't have it!—Throw them into prison!—Freeze them into ice blocks!—Get rid of them! I WANT THAT BEARD!!!!
Queen Billiam dear, if you keep the beard, may I have the talking bird?
King Be quiet, Glary!—That beard will not be safe for one moment if these creatures are free!—Jailor, lock them up instantly!
Thomas You're making a great deal of fuss about a beard!

The Courtroom looks at Thomas in astonished and open-mouthed silence

Why don't you grow one of your own?

The Plutonians gasp

Queen (*fixing Thomas with a steely eye*) That is a *very* badly behaved boy!—Take no notice of that boy, Billiam. That boy needs a good thrashing and putting to bed without supper!
King (*very upset*) He needn't have asked *that* question!—That's a beastly question to ask!—Everyone *knows* I can't grow a beard. Everyone knows that Plutonians can't grow beards!—He needn't have asked *that* question!
Thomas (*going over to the King*) Can't you really? That's very interesting. Something to do with the climate, I suppose.
King Take this boy away, he's staring at me!
Queen He had better *not* be!
Josephine (*going across to the King*) This is my brother, Thomas. He doesn't *mean* to be rude—he's just interested.—Anyway *I* think it's a lot of fuss to make about someone else's beard—it couldn't possibly grow on *you*!—And it would fall to bits if you cut it off.
King Now *she's* saying it!
Rekelen These children speak the truth. The beard belonging to Father

Time is his alone, and can belong to no-one else. Release him at once so that we may all return to Earth.
Queen What? Another talking bird?
King But I *must* have a beard!
Thomas That's easy. If we give you a beard, will you give us Father Time?
King *You* could give me a beard?
Thomas Yes, right away.
Charlotte Thomas, be careful what you say!
Queen Ignore that boy, Billiam, he speaks, untruths!
Thomas I *don't!*
King Show me the beard!
Thomas *You* show *us* Father Time!
Queen Don't do it, Billiam, it's a trap!

The King walks about for a moment thinking hard

King Bring in the Earth prisoner!

The court is in an uproar. The Jailor and his Mother hurry out

Charlotte (*quietly to Thomas*) But Thomas, we haven't got a beard to give to the King.
Thomas Yes we have. It's the Parcel Woman's beard that Hickory wore. I lost mine in the goblin dance, but he still has his.
Hickory (*excitedly*) Of course, I'd forgotten it!—I put it in the Time Box.
Thomas Don't bring it out until we've got Father Time.

The Jailor and his Mother re-enter

Jailor The Earth Prisoner, your Majesty.

Father Time has been brought in. He is bound with silver chains that are hung with great pieces of Plutonium rock

Hickory (*going to him*) Father Time—it *is* you!
Father Time Ah, Hickory, my lad. I knew you would come! I knew I could rely on you.
Hickory But why are you chained like this?
Father Time To keep me from using my Time Power to return to you on Earth. These great crystals contain a radioactive element which neutralizes my power and keeps me chained to this planet.
Hickory (*putting out a hand to touch the chains*) The devils!
King Stand back!—No bargain until I see the beard!

Hickory opens the Time Box and brings forth the white beard

King (*touching it with his finger*) Beautiful, beautiful! But how will it fix on to my chin?
Hickory Like this. (*He hooks the beard over the King's ears*)

Act II, Scene 5   47

Everyone goes into transports of admiration

King A beard of my own, at last!—Release the prisoner!
The Jailor releases the chains and Father Time moves over to the rescue party

Hickory And now; home!—We need no dandelion clocks this time!
Queen Don't let the golden bird get away!
The Plutonians begin to surround the Earth party just as Father Time raises his scythe

Father Time PROCEDETE TEMPUS HORAEQUE UT REDIAMUS AD TERRAM!
All the clocks in the world begin to tick, the Queen cries "save the golden bird"—and they whirl away into blackness

Scene 5

THE CLOCK LABYRINTH

Sitting on the cubes, and completely at home, are the Mice. Each has a napkin tied firmly around its neck and each is tucking into food which is piled high on a dinner plate and balanced on its lap. Mrs Ariadne Time hovers anxiously amongst them with a serving-dish and spoon

Mrs Ariadne (*temptingly, to a small mouse*) A few more peas? They're fresh, you know. Grown in our own garden.
The Small Mouse (*rudely*) All right then. May as well finish them up. Shovel 'em on!

Mrs Ariadne shovels 'em on, and moves to another mouse who is shouting with his mouth rather disgustingly full

Another Mouse More sausage!—More sausage!
Mrs Ariadne (*hurrying to him*) Just coming!—One or two?
Another Mouse Can't you make it three?
Mrs Ariadne Well I thought perhaps somebody else might want one.
Another Mouse Never mind "somebody else"! I want three. I shouted first!
Mrs Ariadne (*serving three sausages*) There you are.
Another Mouse That's better. And next time make them more crisp on the outside!

The other Mice are shouting for things like "bread and butter" and "barley wine" and "where's the tomato sauce?"

Mrs Ariadne (*producing bread and tomato sauce from her tray*) There you are—I'll just fetch the barley wine from the cellar.
A Third Mouse And don't be too long about it!
A Fourth Mouse And make certain it isn't corked!
A Fifth Mouse And see that the glasses are clean!

A Sixth Mouse And be sure they're *big* glasses!
Mrs Ariadne Of course.

She is hurrying out to do their bidding when she sees the Parcel Woman sitting on a cube and knitting furiously

Parcel Woman A rod for your own back—that's what you're making. A rod for your own back.
Mrs Ariadne That's enough from you, Parcel Woman. You mind your own business, I'll mind mine!
Parcel Woman Making fools of mice. Whoever heard of mice eating sausages?
Mrs Ariadne I'm warning you, Parcel Woman!—I'm warning you!
Parcel Woman *And* knives and forks!
Mrs Ariadne Keep your tongue still, you Parcel Woman, you! I'm warning you!
Parcel Woman And *I'm* warning *you*, Mrs Time! You're making fools of those mice. Each should be to its own place, Mrs Time. Each within its own capacity. Each inside its own parcel, you might say. Why, I don't put the fish-bones into the same parcel as I put the cowslips! It wouldn't do! You're mixing for trouble, Mrs Time, that's what you're doing!
Mrs Ariadne (*beginning to cry*) I only want a bit of company, that's all I want. It's lonely in the back of the clock without Father Time and Hickory. No-one to look for. No-one to talk to.
Parcel Woman You never made provision, Mrs Time, that's your trouble! You never stored up a cupboard full of parcels for your old age!
Mrs Ariadne You and your parcels!
Parcel Woman Don't you go scoffing at my parcels, Mrs Time. I can always open a parcel or two when I'm a bit down. Parcels is a comfort, Mrs Time.

The Mice are becoming noisy again, banging their forks on their plates, and shouting "We want barley wine, we want barley wine!"

Mrs Ariadne (*unhappily*) They *are* getting a bit out of hand.
Parcel Woman Don't you serve them, Mrs Time. They're rude, ungrateful beasts, them mice!
Mrs Ariadne Yes, they are. I can see it now.
Parcel Woman Don't you give them no more of anything.
Mrs Ariadne (*making up her mind to be firm*) I won't!
Parcel Woman You sit quiet here, along with me, and wrap up a parcel.
Mrs Ariadne I think I will.
Parcel Woman Here's a bit of brown paper and string. That'll give you a start.
Mrs Ariadne That's a kind thought, Parcel Woman. That's a neighbourly gesture. (*She looks helplessly at the paper*) But, I don't know what to put in a parcel.
Parcel Woman Look around, Mrs Time. There's always something. A few dried leaves, maybe, the colour of copper. A piece of a spider's web

that's been touched by the frost. A handful of dust caught in a shaft of sunlight. There's always something, if you look.

The Mice are becoming louder and beastlier. They begin moving towards Mrs Ariadne, shouting and shrieking for barley wine. At the height of the noise there is a shrill blast on the whistle, and Hickory appears on the top of a cube. The Mice are instantly silent

Hickory (*in a voice to inspire terror in the toughest mouse*) What's this I see?—*Mice* in the back of the clock?
Mrs Ariadne (*ashamed of her weakness*) I'm afraid so, Dock.
Hickory *Mice* rampaging all over the cog wheels?
Mrs Ariadne (*miserably*) They won't go away.
Hickory They shall be *made* to go away, Mrs Time. Just you watch this!!

Hickory goes into a masterly rendering of the mouse-frightening routine, and, screaming wildly, the Mice flee from the labyrinth

Mrs Ariadne Oh, Dock, I *am* glad to see you back!
Hickory And not just me, Mrs Ariadne. Look!

Hickory steps back and Father Time moves into the labyrinth

Mrs Ariadne (*wild with delight*) He's back!!—You've brought him back!—Here's a blessed day for the whole world!

Father Time comes forward and takes her hands

Father Time I'm afraid you have been very worried about me, Ariadne.
Mrs Ariadne Think nothing of it.
Father Time And lonely, I shouldn't wonder.
Mrs Ariadne Yes, my dear. But—but I had the Parcel Woman, you know. (*She looks shyly at the Parcel Woman*)
Parcel Woman That's right. I'm always here if I'm wanted.
Father Time Listen!

He holds up his hand and we hear the gentle, rhythmic sound of the clocks of the world ticking

Mrs Ariadne What a golden sound.
Parcel Woman Yes, indeed. Might be worth putting into a parcel.
Father Time The tides of the world are flowing again, and the moon sails smoothly in its appointed place.
Mrs Ariadne How clever of you, Hickory, to find him.
Hickory You forget, Mrs Ariadne, I had help.

He waves his hand towards the three children who are standing at the back of the labyrinth and are now dressed in their jeans and sweaters

Father Time Indeed, without these children from the other side of the clock, nothing could have been accomplished. It was this boy who told Hickory of dandelion time!
Mrs Ariadne He's a good boy. I said so from the very beginning. Didn't I say, Hickory, what a good boy he was?
Hickory Listen!—I think I've heard that sound before. (*A very familiar clattering and clanking can be heard*) Quick!—They're coming for him again! Stand Back!!

Everyone crowds protectively around Father Time

Frod clanks in

Thomas It's one of the Plutonians!
Hickory Go on!—Off with you!!—We gave your King a beard, what do you want now???

Hickory and Thomas try to push Frod away. Frod trips and falls with a great clanking of tins

Charlotte Oh, don't hurt him! I'm sure he doesn't want to harm anyone!
Frod That's right, I don't want to do no harm. I just come back for the tin-opener, that's all!
Charlotte (*going across to him*) Let me help you up.

She helps Frod to his feet

Frod Thank you, miss. You're kind, you are. I said to Harley "I'll go back for the tin-opener. One of the young ladies is ever so kind," I said. "She'll tell you the way to the Post Office if you ask her," I said. And she's got pretty hair, too.
Josephine Do you *want* to know the way to the Post Office?
Frod No, miss, not really. What I really wants is the tin-opener. Harley thought *I* had it, but I never. It was Binjer what had it. And then Binjer whopped this golden bird on the head with it, and after that we lost track of it because we was looking for the little primus stove!—Well, the little primus stove was all right, because Till had it, but we never got given no matches. Nobody never thought of giving us none!—So Harley says I mustn't go back without it.
Hickory (*rather confused*) Without what?
Frod (*gloomily*) The tin-opener. And I've looked everywhere!—It's not in that circus where you went. Nor it isn't under the sea. I got to the Goblin place but they shouted at me so much I come away!—Then I went to the top of that mountain, but they're all busy up there watching the golden bird lighting a bonfire, so I come back here. Harley says I mustn't go back without it, and I *would* like to try the tomato soup!

Harley tip-toes on and hisses at Frod

Harley Pssst!—Frod!!

Act II, Scene 5

Frod What?
Harley We found it.
Frod What?
Harley The tin-opener. Dred had it.
Frod I thought Dred had the torch?
Harley Dred *did* have the torch, but he left it behind. (*Impatiently*) Come on, Frod, they've got the little primus stove going, and we're waiting for the tomato soup!
Frod (*looking at his tins*) I think I've crushed the tomato soup, Harley.
Harley You had *two* tomato soups, there's one hanging round your neck! —Now come on!
Frod Righto, Harley.

They start to go

Harley And Frod . . .
Frod Yes?
Harley Watch the noise!
Frod Sorry, Harley.

Harley and Frod (clanking) go off

Father Time And now there is work to be done. Everything must be cleaned and oiled, and these children must be returned to their own time and place.—Hickory, take them to the door of the clock.

Everyone says good-bye to the children and they disappear into the shadows with Hickory

The ticking of the clocks becomes louder

Father Time Come along, Ariadne, my dear, don't let us waste time just as we have got it back! What are you thinking of, sitting there like some graven image?

The music of time swells to a crescendo as:

the CURTAIN *falls*

FURNITURE AND PROPERTY LIST

In addition to the seven cubes already mentioned we list below the *minimum* requirements for properties, etc. Other pieces can be added at the producer's discretion.

ACT I

Scene 1

On stage: Round table. *On it:* dark cloth
Grandfather clock
Game of Ludo with cup and dice

Personal: **Hickory:** black Time Box

Scene 2

Off stage: Parcel containing five dandelion clocks (**Parcel Woman**)

Personal: **Parcel Woman:** knitting

Scene 3

Set: Twigs behind a cube, down left

Personal: **Mrs Noah:** basket of washing

Scene 4

Off stage: Large admission tickets (**all Goblins**)
Parcel containing two white beards (**Rekelen**)

Personal: **Glumm and Goatnose:** small wicket gate
Gooseberry: besom, ticket-punching machine
Frod: phrase book

ACT II

Scene 1

Personal: **Goose Woman:** sack
North Wind: sack

Scene 2

Personal: **Three Sailors:** a bucket and a cutlass each
Plutonians: aerosols

Scene 3

Set: Sawdust on floor
Piece of tinsel

Scene 4

Personal: **Clerk of Court:** large lump of silver rock

Scene 5

Set: Plates of food, knives and forks
Serving-dishes and spoons

Personal: **Parcel Woman:** piece of brown paper and string

LIGHTING PLOT

Property fittings required: nil

ACT I, SCENE 1. A room
To open: Gloomy lighting with effect of lamp through "window"
No cues

ACT I, SCENE 2. The Clock Labyrinth
To open: Shadowy lighting
Cue 1 At end of scene after music ceases (Page 14)
  Bright sunshine

ACT I, SCENE 3. The Mountain
To open: Bright sunshine
No cues

ACT I, SCENE 4. Land of the Goblins
To open: Bright, airy lighting
Cue 2 As **Thomas** reaches gate (Page 27)
  Moonlight goes and darkness descends

ACT II, SCENE 1. Land of Limbo
To open: Grey lighting
No cues

ACT II, SCENE 2. Beneath the Ocean
To open: Mood lighting
No cues

ACT II, SCENE 3. Circus
To open: Blue light streaming to centre of ring
Cue 3 **Third Woman:** "Why, there's nothing easier!" (Page 39)
  Yellow lights come up
Cue 4 Circus people move away (Page 40)
  Yellow lights fade, leaving previous lighting

ACT II, SCENE 4. Planet Pluto
To open: Mood lighting
No cues

ACT II, SCENE 5. The Clock Labyrinth
To open: Shadowy lighting
No cues

EFFECTS PLOT

ACT I
Scene 1

Cue 1	As **Charlotte** shakes cup *Handbell and man's voice in street*	(Page 1)
Cue 2	**Josephine** ". . . or get another out?" *Bell and voice grow louder. Cart wheels and horses outside*	(Page 1)
Cue 3	**Thomas**: ". . . your hair all different!" *Horse and carriage draw up outside*	(Page 2)
Cue 4	**Charlotte**: "That's what *I* want to know!" *Muddled half-hour chime*	(Page 3)
Cue 5	**Mrs Ariadne** sobs bitterly *Muddled three-quarters chime*	(Page 4)
Cue 6	**Hickory**: ". . . into the Clock Labyrinth." *Loud slow ticking and Music of Time, ceasing as scene change ends*	(Page 6)

Scene 2

Cue 7	**Josephine**: ". . . more a clicking kind of noise." *Clicking noise*	(Page 7)
Cue 8	After a moment of silence in the labyrinth *Loud clattering noise and voices*	(Page 9)
Cue 9	**Hickory**: "To the mountain!" *Slow ticking and Music of Time*	(Page 14)

Scene 3

Cue 10	As Scene opens *Marching, singing and rattle of tins*	(Page 14)
Cue 11	As dandelion seeds blow in air *Clock ticks and Music of Time*	(Page 21)

Scene 4

Cue 12	To open *Goblin music*	(Page 21)
Cue 13	**Glumm**: ". . . none too good at dancing." *Goblin music ends and silver horn sounds*	(Page 21)
Cue 14	**Hickory**: ". . . but could I . . . ?" *Silver trumpet sounds*	(Page 22)
Cue 15	**Herald**: "Come one! Come all!" *Trumpet sounds*	(Page 22)
Cue 16	**Glumm**: ". . . what rabbit holes are like!" *Goblin music*	(Page 26)

ACT II

Scene 1

Cue 17	**Rescue party** peer into gloom *Muffled cries of sea birds*	(Page 28)
Cue 18	North wind lets snow go from his sack *Great clock ticks and Music of Time*	(Page 31)

Scene 2

Cue 19	**Hickory:** "One, two, three, BLOW!" *Clock ticks and Music of Time*	(Page 37)

Scene 3

Cue 20	Yellow lights come up *Brassy circus music*	(Page 39)
Cue 21	Circus people move away *Music fades*	(Page 40)
Cue 22	**Hickory:** "One, two, three BLOW!" *Clock ticks and Music of Time*	(Page 41)

Scene 4

Cue 23	**Father Time:** ". . . *rediamus ad terram!*" *Clock begins to tick*	(Page 47)

Scene 5

Cue 24	**Father Time:** "Listen!" *Clocks ticking*	(Page 49)
Cue 25	Children disappear *Ticking gets louder, Music of Time swells*	(Page 51)

www.ingramcontent.com/pod-product-compliance
Ingram Content Group UK Ltd.
Pitfield, Milton Keynes, MK11 3LW, UK
UKHW021847210426
5322IPUK00022B/519